R. Murray

CLARENDON ARISTOTLE SERIES

General Editors

J. L. ACKRILL AND LINDSAY JUDSON

D1570057

ARISTOTLE
Categories and
De Interpretatione

Translated with Notes
by
J. L. ACKRILL

CLARENDON PRESS · OXFORD

This book has been printed digitally and produced in a standard specification
in order to ensure its continuing availability

OXFORD
UNIVERSITY PRESS

Great Clarendon Street, Oxford OX2 6DP

Oxford University Press is a department of the University of Oxford.
It furthers the University's objective of excellence in research, scholarship,
and education by publishing worldwide in

Oxford New York

Auckland Bangkok Buenos Aires Cape Town Chennai
Dar es Salaam Delhi Hong Kong Istanbul Karachi Kolkata
Kuala Lumpur Madrid Melbourne Mexico City Mumbai Nairobi
São Paulo Shanghai Singapore Taipei Tokyo Toronto
with an associated company in Berlin

Oxford is a registered trade mark of Oxford University Press
in the UK and in certain other countries

Published in the United States
by Oxford University Press Inc., New York

ISBN 0-19-872086-6

PREFACE

THE main purpose of this work is to provide a translation of Aristotle's *Categories* and *De Interpretatione* that shall be of service to the serious student of philosophy who does not read Greek. The existing English versions are not well suited to the needs of such a reader: they are not sufficiently literal, and they do not attempt to preserve consistency in the rendering of key terms. The present translation sticks more closely to the original in order to enable the Greekless reader to exercise his own judgement on questions of interpretation.

The text translated is that of the best and most recent edition, L. Minio-Paluello's edition in the Oxford Classical Texts Series (1949, with corrections 1956). But I have omitted the lines 2ᵇ6–6ᵉ (which are a mere repetition of 2ᵇ3–6), I have adopted variant readings at 1ᵇ16, 16ᵇ22, 18ᵇ21, 18ᵇ22, and 21ᵃ14; and I have introduced conjectural emendations at 8ᵇ19 and 15ᵃ16.

There is no English commentary on the *Categories* and *De Interpretatione*, and no recent commentary in any language. The notes in this volume do not pretend to the status of a commentary. Limited in scope and elementary in character, they are offered only as an aid to beginners. In the absence of any other chapter-by-chapter discussion of the works it has seemed desirable to write fairly full notes on individual passages, even though this has made it impossible to include a synoptic introduction containing a general examination of major topics. The philosophical questions treated in, or raised by, the *Categories* and *De Interpretatione* are so numerous and difficult that a short introductory discussion would have been worthless; and an adequate one would have left little or no space for notes on particular passages.

The Glossary indicates what renderings have been adopted for certain important Greek terms. The Index is necessarily selective, but it aims at giving references to all passages likely to be of interest in connexion with the topics listed.

I am indebted to many friends and colleagues for helpful discussion about problems in the *Categories* and *De Interpretatione*. I am conscious of having benefited particularly from a class given at Oxford in 1956–7 by the late J. L. Austin and Mr. H. P. Grice. Mr. Richard Robinson kindly read a draft of the translation of the *Categories* and made valuable suggestions. Just before I made my final revision of the *De Interpretatione* translation, Mr. E. J. Lemmon kindly gave me a copy of a translation he had made. I was happy to find that our versions were in general very similar, but I was able to make some improvements to mine as a result of studying his. Mr. M. J. Woods has helped in the correcting of proofs, and has made some very useful suggestions.

I am grateful to Brasenose College for granting me the sabbatical leave during which this book was written. I am grateful to the Institute for Advanced Study at Princeton for enabling me to do the writing in ideal conditions, and to Professor Harold Cherniss for his kindness and help there.

J. L. A.

Brasenose College, Oxford
April 1963

CONTENTS

TRANSLATION

CATEGORIES

1ᵃ1. When things have only a name in common and the definition of being which corresponds to the name is different, they are called *homonymous*. Thus, for example, both a man and a picture are animals. These have only a name in common and the definition of being which corresponds to the name is different; for if one is to say what being an animal is for each of them, one will give two distinct definitions.

1ᵃ6. When things have the name in common and the definition of being which corresponds to the name is the same, they are called *synonymous*. Thus, for example, both a man and an ox are animals. Each of these is called by a common name, 'animal', and the definition of being is also the same; for if one is to give the definition of each—what being an animal is for each of them—one will give the same definition.

1ᵃ12. When things get their name from something, with a difference of ending, they are called *paronymous*. Thus, for example, the grammarian gets his name from grammar, the brave get theirs from bravery.

CHAPTER 2

1ᵃ16. Of things that are said, some involve combination while others are said without combination. Examples of those involving combination are 'man runs', 'man wins'; and of those without combination 'man', 'ox', 'runs', 'wins'.

1ª20. Of things there are: (*a*) some are *said of* a subject but are not *in* any subject. For example, man is said of a subject, the individual man, but is not in any subject. (*b*) Some are in a subject but are not said of any subject. (By 'in a subject' I mean what is in something, not as a part, and cannot exist separately from what it is in.) For example, the individual knowledge-of-grammar is in a subject, the soul, but is not said of any subject; and the individual white is in a subject, the body (for all colour is in a body), but is not said of any subject. (*c*) Some are both said of a subject and in a subject. For example, knowledge is in a subject, the soul, and is also said of a subject, knowledge-of-grammar. (*d*) Some are neither in a subject nor said of a subject, for example, the individual man or individual horse—for nothing of this sort is either in a subject or said of a subject. Things that are individual and numerically one are, without exception, not said of any subject, but there is nothing to prevent some of them from being in a subject—the individual knowledge-of-grammar is one of the things in a subject.

CHAPTER 3

1ᵇ10. Whenever one thing is predicated of another as of a subject, all things said of what is predicated will be said of the subject also. For example, man is predicated of the individual man, and animal of man; so animal will be predicated of the individual man also—for the individual man is both a man and an animal.

1ᵇ16. The differentiae of genera which are different[1] and not subordinate one to the other are themselves different in kind. For example, animal and knowledge: footed, winged, aquatic, two-footed, are differentiae of animal,

---

[1] Read τῶν ἑτέρων γενῶν.

but none of these is a differentia of knowledge; one sort of knowledge does not differ from another by being two-footed. However, there is nothing to prevent genera subordinate one to the other from having the same differentiae. For the higher are predicated of the genera below them, so that all differentiae of the predicated genus will be differentiae of the subject also.

CHAPTER 4

1^b25. Of things said without any combination, each signifies either substance or quantity or qualification or a relative or where or when or being-in-a-position or having or doing or being-affected. To give a rough idea, examples of substance are man, horse; of quantity: four-foot, five-foot; of qualification: white, grammatical; of a relative: double, half, larger; of where: in the Lyceum, in the market-place; of when: yesterday, last-year; of being-in-a-position: is-lying, is-sitting; of having: has-shoes-on, has-armour-on; of doing: cutting, burning; of being-affected: being-cut, being-burned.

2^a4. None of the above is said just by itself in any affirmation, but by the combination of these with one another an affirmation is produced. For every affirmation, it seems, is either true or false; but of things said without any combination none is either true or false (e.g. 'man', 'white', 'runs', 'wins').

CHAPTER 5

2^a11. A *substance*—that which is called a substance most strictly, primarily, and most of all—is that which is neither said of a subject nor in a subject, e.g. the individual man or the individual horse. The species in which the things primarily called substances are, are called *secondary substances*, as also are the genera of these species. For example, the individual man belongs in a species, man, and animal is a genus of the species; so these—both man and animal—are called secondary substances.

2ᵃ19. It is clear from what has been said that if something is said of a subject both its name and its definition are necessarily predicated of the subject. For example, man is said of a subject, the individual man, and the name is of course predicated (since you will be predicating man of the individual man), and also the definition of man will be predicated of the individual man (since the individual man is also a man). Thus both the name and the definition will be predicated of the subject. But as for things which are in a subject, in most cases neither the name nor the definition is predicated of the subject. In some cases there is nothing to prevent the name from being predicated of the subject, but it is impossible for the definition to be predicated. For example, white, which is in a subject (the body), is predicated of the subject; for a body is called white. But the definition of white will never be predicated of the body.

2ᵃ34. All the other things are either said of the primary substances as subjects or in them as subjects. This is clear from an examination of cases. For example, animal is predicated of man and therefore also of the individual man; for were it predicated of none of the individual men it would not be predicated of man at all. Again, colour is in body and therefore also in an individual body; for were it not in some individual body it would not be in body at all. Thus all the other things are either said of the primary substances as subjects or in them as subjects. So if the primary substances did not exist it would be impossible for any of the other things to exist.

2^b7. Of the secondary substances the species is more a substance than the genus, since it is nearer to the primary substance. For if one is to say of the primary substance what it is, it will be more informative and apt to give the species than the genus. For example, it would be more informative to say of the individual man that he is a man than that he is an animal (since the one is more distinctive of the individual man while the other is more general); and more informative to say of the individual tree that it is a tree than that it is a plant. Further, it is because the primary substances are subjects for all the other things and all the other things are predicated of them or are in them, that they are called substances most of all. But as the primary substances stand to the other things, so the species stands to the genus: the species is a subject for the genus (for the genera are predicated of the species but the species are not predicated reciprocally of the genera). Hence for this reason too the species is more a substance than the genus.

2^b22. But of the species themselves—those which are not genera—one is no more a substance than another: it is no more apt to say of the individual man that he is a man than to say of the individual horse that it is a horse. And similarly of the primary substances one is no more a substance than another: the individual man is no more a substance than the individual ox.

2^b29. It is reasonable that, after the primary substances, their species and genera should be the only other things called (secondary) substances. For only they, of things predicated, reveal the primary substance. For if one is to say of the individual man what he is, it will be in place to give the species or the genus (though more informative to give man than animal); but to give any of the other things would be out of place—for example, to say 'white' or 'runs' or anything like that. So it is reasonable that these should be the only other things called substances. Further, it is because the primary substances are subjects for everything else that they are called substances most strictly. But as the primary substances stand to everything else, so the species and genera of the primary substances stand to all the rest: all the rest are predicated of these. For if you will call the individual man grammatical it follows that you will call both a man and an animal grammatical; and similarly in other cases.

3ᵃ7 It is a characteristic common to every substance not to be in a subject. For a primary substance is neither said of a subject nor in a subject. And as for secondary substances, it is obvious at once that they are not in a subject. For man is said of the individual man as subject but is not in a subject: man is not *in* the individual man. Similarly, animal also is said of the individual man as subject but animal is not *in* the individual man. Further, while there is nothing to prevent the name of what is in a subject from being sometimes predicated of the subject, it is impossible for the definition to be predicated. But the definition of the secondary substances, as well as the name, is predicated of the subject: you will predicate the definition of man of the individual man, and also that of animal. No substance, therefore, is in a subject.

3ᵃ21. This is not, however, peculiar to substance; the differentia also is not in a subject. For footed and two-footed are said of man as subject but are not in a subject; neither two-footed nor footed is *in* man. Moreover, the definition of the differentia is predicated of that of which the differentia is said. For example, if footed is said of man the definition of footed will also be predicated of man; for man is footed.

3ª29. We need not be disturbed by any fear that we may be forced to say that the parts of a substance, being in a subject (the whole substance), are not substances. For when we spoke of things *in a subject* we did not mean things belonging in something as *parts*.

3ª33. It is a characteristic of substances and differentiae that all things called from them are so called synonymously. For all the predicates from them are predicated either of the individuals or of the species. (For from a primary substance there is no predicate, since it is said of no subject; and as for secondary substances, the species is predicated of the individual, the genus both of the species and of the individual. Similarly, differentiae too are predicated both of the species and of the individuals.) And the primary substances admit the definition of the species and of the genera, and the species admits that of the genus; for everything said of what is predicated will be said of the subject also. Similarly, both the species and the individuals admit the definition of the differentiae. But synonymous things were precisely those with both the name in common and the same definition. Hence all the things called from substances and differentiae are so called synònymously.

3ᵇ10. Every substance seems to signify a certain 'this'. As regards the primary substances, it is indisputably true that each of them signifies a certain 'this'; for the thing revealed is individual and numerically one. But as regards the secondary substances, though it appears from the form of the name—when one speaks of man or animal—that a secondary substance likewise signifies a certain 'this', this is not really true; rather, it signifies a certain qualification, for the subject is not, as the primary substance is, one, but man and animal are said of many things.

However, it does not signify simply a certain qualification, as white does. White signifies nothing but a qualification, whereas the species and the genus mark off the qualification of substance—they signify substance of a certain qualification. (One draws a wider boundary with the genus than with the species, for in speaking of animal one takes in more than in speaking of man.)

3ᵇ24. Another characteristic of substances is that there is nothing contrary to them. For what would be contrary to a primary substance? For example, there is nothing contrary to an individual man, nor yet is there anything contrary to man or to animal. This, however, is not peculiar to substance but holds of many other things also, for example, of quantity. For there is nothing contrary to four-foot or to ten or to anything of this kind—unless someone were to say that many is contrary to few or large to small; but still there is nothing contrary to any *definite* quantity.

3ᵇ33. Substance, it seems, does not admit of a more and a less. I do not mean that one substance is not more a substance than another (we have said that it is), but that any given substance is not called more, or less, that which it is. For example, if this substance is a man, it will not be more a man or less a man either than itself or than another man. For one man is not more a man than another, as one pale thing is more pale than another and one beautiful thing more beautiful than another. Again, a thing is called more, or less, such-and-such than itself; for example, the body that is pale is called more pale now than before, and the one that is hot is called more, or less, hot. Substance, however, is not spoken of thus. For a man is not called more a man now than before, nor is anything else that is a substance. Thus substance does not admit of a more and a less.

4ᵃ10. It seems most distinctive of substance that what is numerically one and the same is able to receive contraries. In no other case could one bring forward anything, numerically one, which is able to receive contraries. For example, a colour which is numerically one and the same will not be black and white, nor will numerically one and the same action be bad and good; and similarly with everything else that is not substance. A substance, however, numerically one and the same, is able to receive contraries. For example, an individual man—one and the same—becomes pale at one time and dark at another, and hot and cold, and bad and good. Nothing like this is to be seen in any other case.

4ᵃ22. But perhaps someone might object and say that statements and beliefs are like this. For the same statement seems to be both true and false. Suppose, for example, that the statement that somebody is sitting is true; after he has got up this same statement will be false. Similarly with beliefs. Suppose you believe truly that somebody is sitting; after he has got up you will believe falsely if you hold the same belief about him. However, even if we were to grant this, there is still a difference in the *way* contraries are received. For in the case of substances it is by themselves changing that they are able to receive contraries. For what has become cold instead of hot, or dark instead of pale, or good instead of bad, has changed (has altered); similarly in other cases too it is by itself undergoing change that each thing is able to receive contraries. Statements and beliefs, on the other hand, themselves remain completely unchangeable in every way; it is because the *actual thing* changes that the contrary comes to belong to them. For the statement that somebody is sitting remains the same; it is because of a change in the actual thing that it comes to be true at one time and false at another. Similarly with beliefs. Hence at least the *way* in which it is able to receive contraries—through a change in itself—would be distinctive of substance, even if we were to grant that beliefs and statements are able to receive contraries. However, this is not true. For it is not because they themselves receive anything that statements and beliefs are said to be able to receive contraries, but because of what has happened to something else. For it is because the actual thing exists or does not exist that the statement is said to be true or false, not because it is able itself to receive contraries. No statement, in fact, or belief is changed at all by anything. So, since nothing happens in them, they are not able to receive contraries. A substance, on the other hand, is said to be able to receive contraries because it itself receives contraries. For it receives sickness and health, and paleness and darkness; and because it itself receives the various things of this kind it is said to be able to receive contraries. It is, therefore, distinctive of substance that what is numerically one and the same is able to receive contraries. This brings to an end our discussion of substance.

CHAPTER 6

4^b20. Of quantities some are discrete, others continuous; and some are composed of parts which have position in relation to one another, others are not composed of parts which have position.

4^b22. Discrete are number and language; continuous are lines, surfaces, bodies, and also, besides these, time and place. For the parts of a number have no common boundary at which they join together. For example, if five is a part of ten the two fives do not join together at any common boundary but are separate; nor do the three and the seven join together at any common boundary. Nor could you ever in the case of a number find a common boundary of its parts, but they are always separate. Hence number is one of the discrete quantities. Similarly, language also is one of the discrete quantities (that language is a quantity is evident, since it is measured by long and short syllables; I mean here language that is *spoken*). For its parts do not join together at any common boundary. For there is no common boundary at which the syllables join together, but each is separate in itself. A line, on the other hand, is a continuous quantity. For it is possible to find a common boundary at which its parts join together, a point. And for a surface, a line; for the parts of a plane join together at some common boundary. Similarly in the case of a body one could find a common boundary —a line or a surface—at which the parts of the body join together. Time also and place are of this kind. For present time joins on to both past time and future time. Place, again, is one of the continuous quantities. For the parts of a body occupy some place, and they join together at a common boundary. So the parts of the place occupied by the various parts of the body, themselves join together at the same boundary at which the parts of the body do. Thus place also is a continuous quantity, since its parts join together at one common boundary.

5ª15. Further, some quantities are composed of parts which have position in relation to one another, others are not composed of parts which have position. For example, the parts of a line have position in relation to one another; each of them is situated somewhere, and you could distinguish them and say where each is situated in the plane and which one of the other parts it joins on to. Similarly, the parts of a plane have some position; here again one could say where each is situated and which join on to one another. So, too, with the parts of a solid and the parts of a place. With a number, on the other hand, one could not observe that the parts have some position in relation to one another or are situated somewhere, nor see which of the parts join on to one another. Nor with the parts of a time either; for none of the parts of a time endures, and how could what is not enduring have any position? Rather might you say that they have a certain *order* in that one part of a time is before and another after. Similarly with a number also, in that one is counted before two and two before three; in this way they may have a certain order, but you would certainly not find position. And language similarly. For none of its parts endures, once it has been uttered it can no longer be recaptured; and so its parts cannot have position, seeing that none of them endures. Some quantities then are composed of parts which have position, others are not composed of parts which have position.

5ᵃ38. Only these we have mentioned are called quantities strictly, all the others derivatively; for it is to these we look when we call the others quantities. For example, we speak of a large amount of white because the *surface* is large, and an action or a change is called long because the *time* is long. For it is not in its own right that each of these others is called a quantity. For example, if one is to say how long an action is, one will determine this by the time, saying that it is a-year-long or something of that sort; and in saying how much white one will determine it by the surface—whatever the size of the surface one will say that the white too is that size. Thus only those we mentioned are called quantities strictly and in their own right, while nothing else is so in its own right but, if at all, derivatively.

5ᵇ11. Next, a quantity has no contrary. In the case of definite quantities it is obvious that there is no contrary; there is, for example, no contrary to four-foot or five-foot or to a surface or anything like that. But might someone say that many is contrary to few or large to small? None of these, however, is a quantity; they are relatives. For nothing is called large or small just in itself, but by reference to something else. For example, a mountain is called small yet a grain of millet large—because one is larger than other things of its kind while the other is smaller than other things of its kind. Thus the reference is to something else, since if a thing were called small or large in itself the mountain would never be called small yet the grain of millet large. Again, we say that there are many people in the village but few in Athens—though there are many times more here than there; and that there are many in the house but few in the theatre—though there are many more here than there. Further, 'four-foot', 'five-foot', and the like all signify a quantity, but 'large' or 'small' does not signify a quantity but rather a relative, since the large and the small are looked at in relation to something else. So it is clear that these are relatives.

5ᵇ30. Moreover, whether one counts them as quantities or does not, they have no contrary. For how could there be any contrary to what cannot be grasped just in itself but only by reference to something else? Further, if large and small are to be contraries it will turn out that the same thing admits contraries at the same time, and that things are their own contraries. For the same thing turns out to be at the same time both large and small—since in relation to this thing it is small but in relation to another this same thing is large; so the same thing turns out to be both large and small at the same time and thus to admit contraries at the same time. But nothing seems to admit contraries at the same time. In the case of a substance, for example, while it seems to be able to receive contraries, yet it is certainly not at the same time ill and well nor is it at the same time pale and dark; nor does anything else admit contraries at the same time. It turns out also that things are their own contraries. For if large is contrary to small, and the same thing is at the same time large and small, a thing would be its own contrary. But it is impossible for a thing to be its own contrary. Large, therefore, is not contrary to small, nor many to few. So that even if someone says that these belong not to relatives but to quantity, it will still have no contrary.

6ª11. But it is most of all with regard to place that there seems to be contrariety of a quantity. For people regard up as contrary to down—meaning by 'down' the region towards the centre—because the centre is at the greatest distance from the limits of the world. And they probably derive from these their definition of the other contraries also; for they define as contraries those things in the same genus which are most distant from one another.

6ª19. A quantity does not seem to admit of a more and a less. Four-foot for example: one thing is not more four-foot than another. Or take number: we do not speak of a three as more three than a five, nor of one three as more three than another three. Nor yet is one time called more a time than another. Nor is there a single one, among those we listed, as to which a more and a less is spoken of. Hence a quantity does not admit of a more and a less.

6ª26. Most distinctive of a quantity is its being called

both equal and unequal. For each of the quantities we spoke of is called both equal and unequal. For example, a body is called both equal and unequal, and a number is called both equal and unequal, and so is a time; so also with the others we spoke of, each is called both equal and unequal. But anything else—whatever is not a quantity—is certainly not, it would seem, called equal and unequal. For example, a condition is certainly not called equal and unequal, but, rather, similar; and white is certainly not equal and unequal, but similar. Thus most distinctive of a quantity would be its being called both equal and unequal.

CHAPTER 7

6ᵃ36. We call *relatives* all such things as are said to be just what they are, *of* or *than* other things, or in some other way *in relation to* something else. For example, what is larger is called what it is *than* something else (it is called larger than something); and what is double is called what it is *of* something else (it is called double of something); similarly with all other such cases. The following, too, and their like, are among relatives: state, condition, perception, knowledge, position. For each of these is called what it is (and not something different) *of* something else. A state is called a state of something, knowledge knowledge of something, position position of something, and the rest similarly. All things then are relative which are called just what they are, *of* or *than* something else—or in some other way *in relation to* something else. Thus a mountain is called large in relation to something else (the mountain is called large in relation to something); and what is similar is called similar *to* something; and the others of this kind are in the same way spoken of in relation to something.

6^b11. Lying, standing, and sitting are particular positions; position is a relative. To-be-lying, to-be-standing, or to-be-sitting are themselves not positions, but they get their names paronymously from the aforesaid positions.

6^b15. There is contrariety in relatives, e.g. virtue is contrary to vice (and each of them is relative), and knowledge to ignorance. But there is not a contrary to every relative; there is no contrary to what is double or treble or anything like that.

6^b19. Relatives seem also to admit of a more and a less. For a thing is called more similar and less similar, and more unequal and less unequal; and each of these is relative, since what is similar is called similar *to* something and what is unequal unequal *to* something. But not all admit of a more and less; for what is double, or anything like that, is not called more double or less double.

6^b28. All relatives are spoken of in relation to correlatives that reciprocate. For example, the slave is called slave of a master and the master is called master of a slave; the double double of a half, and the half half of a double; the larger larger than a smaller, and the smaller smaller than a larger; and so for the rest too. Sometimes, however, there will be a verbal difference, of ending. Thus knowledge is called knowledge *of* what is knowable, and what is knowable knowable *by* knowledge; perception perception *of* the perceptible, and the perceptible perceptible *by* perception.

6^b36. Sometimes, indeed, they will not seem to reciprocate—if a mistake is made and that in relation to which something is spoken of is not given properly. For example, if a wing is given as *of a bird*, *bird of a wing* does not reciprocate; for it has not been given properly in the first place as wing of a bird. For it is not as being a bird that a wing is said to be of it, but as being a winged, since many things that are not birds have wings. Thus if it is given properly there is reciprocation; for example, a wing is wing of a winged and a winged is winged with a wing.

7ᵃ5. It may sometimes be necessary even to invent names, if no name exists in relation to which a thing would be given properly. For example, if a rudder is given as *of a boat*, that is not to give it properly (for it is not as being a boat that a rudder is said to be of it, since there are boats which have not got rudders); and so there is not reciprocation—a boat is not called boat of a rudder. But perhaps it would be given more properly if given thus, that a rudder is rudder of (or somehow else related to) a 'ruddered' (since there is no established name); and now there is reciprocation, if it is given properly—a ruddered is ruddered by a rudder. Similarly in other cases. For example, a head would be more properly given as of a headed than as of an animal, because it is not as being an animal that a thing has a head, since many animals have not got a head. This is perhaps the easiest way to lay hold of things for which there are no established names—if names derived from the original relatives are assigned to their reciprocating correlatives, as in the above case 'winged' was derived from 'wing' and 'ruddered' from 'rudder'.

7ᵃ22. All relatives, then, are spoken of in relation to correlatives that reciprocate, *provided* they are properly given. For, of course, if a relative is given as related to some chance thing and not to just that thing in relation to which it is spoken of, there is not reciprocation. I mean that even with relatives that are admittedly spoken of in relation to correlatives that reciprocate and for which names exist, none reciprocates if a relative is given as related to something accidental and not to just that thing in relation to which it is spoken of. For example, if a slave is given as of—not a master, but—a man or a biped or anything else like that, there is not reciprocation; for it has not been given properly.

7ª31. Again, if that in relation to which a thing is spoken of is properly given, then, when all the other things that are accidental are stripped off and that alone is left to which it was properly given as related, it will always be spoken of in relation to that. For example, if a slave is spoken of in relation to a master, then, when everything accidental to a master is stripped off—like being a biped, capable of knowledge, a man—and there is left only its being a master, a slave will always be spoken of in relation to that. For a slave is called slave of a master. On the other hand, if that in relation to which a thing is spoken of is not properly given, then, when the other things are stripped off and that alone is left to which it was given as related, it will not be spoken of in relation to that. Suppose a slave is given as *of a man* and a wing as *of a bird,* and strip off from man his being a master; a slave will no longer be spoken of in relation to a man, for if there is no master there is no slave either. Similarly, strip off from bird its being winged; a wing will no longer be a relative, for if there is nothing winged neither will there be a wing of anything.

7ᵇ10. One must therefore give as correlative whatever it is properly spoken of in relation to; and if a name already exists it is easy to give this, but if it does not it may be necessary to invent a name. When correlatives are given thus it is clear that all relatives will be spoken of in relation to correlatives that reciprocate.

7^b15. Relatives seem to be simultaneous by nature; and in most cases this is true. For there is at the same time a double and a half, and when there is a half there is a double, and when there is a slave there is a master; and similarly with the others. Also, one carries the other to destruction; for if there is not a double there is not a half, and if there is not a half there is not a double. So too with other such cases. Yet it does not seem to be true of all relatives that they are simultaneous by nature. For the knowable would seem to be prior to knowledge. For as a rule it is of actual things already existing that we acquire knowledge; in few cases, if any, could one find knowledge coming into existence at the same time as what is knowable. Moreover, destruction of the knowable carries knowledge to destruction, but knowledge does not carry the knowable to destruction. For if there is not a knowable there is not knowledge—there will no longer be anything for knowledge to be of—but if there is not knowledge there is nothing to prevent there being a knowable. Take, for example, the squaring of the circle, supposing it to be knowable; knowledge of it does not yet exist but the knowable itself exists. Again, if animal is destroyed there is no knowledge, but there may be many knowables. The case of perception is similar to this; the perceptible seems to be prior to perception. For the destruction of the perceptible carries perception to destruction, but perception does not carry the perceptible to destruction. For perceptions are to do with body and in body, and if the perceptible is destroyed, body too is destroyed (since body is itself a perceptible), and if there is not body, perception too is destroyed; hence the perceptible carries perception to destruction. But perception does not carry the perceptible. For if animal is destroyed perception is destroyed, but there will be something perceptible, such as body, hot, sweet, bitter, and all the other perceptibles. Moreover, perception comes into existence at the same time as what is capable of perceiving—an animal and perception come into existence at the same time—but the perceptible exists even before perception exists; fire and water and so on, of which an animal is itself made up, exist even before there exists an animal at all, or perception. Hence the perceptible would seem to be prior to perception.

8ª13. It is a problem whether (as one would think) *no* substance is spoken of as a relative, or whether this is possible with regard to some secondary substances. In the case of primary substances it is true; neither wholes nor parts are spoken of in relation to anything. An individual man is not called someone's individual man, nor an individual ox someone's individual ox. Similarly with parts; an individual hand is not called someone's individual hand (but someone's hand), and an individual head is not called someone's individual head (but someone's head). Similarly with secondary substances, at any rate most of them. For example, a man is not called someone's man nor an ox someone's ox nor a log someone's log (but it is called someone's property). With such cases, then, it is obvious that they are not relatives, but with some secondary substances there is room for dispute. For example, a head is called someone's head and a hand is called someone's hand, and so on; so that these would seem to be relatives.

8ª28. Now if the definition of relatives which was given above was adequate, it is either exceedingly difficult or impossible to reach the solution that no substance is spoken of as a relative. But if it was not adequate, and if those things are relatives for which *being is the same as being somehow related to something*, then perhaps some answer may be found. The previous definition does, indeed, apply to all relatives, yet this—their being called what they are, of other things—is not what their being relatives is.

8ᵃ35. It is clear from this that if someone knows any relative definitely he will also know definitely that in relation to which it is spoken of. This is obvious on the face of it. For if someone knows of a certain 'this' that it is a relative, and being for relatives is the same as being somehow related to something, he knows that also to which this is somehow related. For if he does not in the least know that to which this is somehow related, neither will he know whether it is somehow related to something. The same point is clear also in particular cases. For example, if someone knows definitely of a certain 'this' that it is double he also, by the same token, knows definitely what it is double of; for if he does not know it to be double anything definite neither does he know whether it is double at all. Similarly, if he knows of a certain 'this' that it is more beautiful, he must also, because of this, know definitely what it is more beautiful than. (He is not to know *indefinitely* that this is more beautiful than an inferior thing. This is a case of supposition, not knowledge. For he will no longer strictly *know* that it is more beautiful than an inferior thing, since it may so happen that there is nothing inferior to it.) It is plain, therefore, that anyone who knows any relative definitely must know definitely that also in relation to which it is spoken of.

8ᵇ15. But as for a head or a hand or any such substance, it is possible to know it—what it itself is—definitely, without necessarily knowing definitely that in relation to which it is spoken of. For whose this head is, or whose the hand, it is not necessary[1] to know definitely. So these would not

---

[1] Read οὐκ ⟨ἀναγκαῖόν⟩ ἐστιν εἰδέναι. The received text says: ' . . . it is not *possible* to know definitely'.

be relatives. And if they are not relatives it would be true to say that no substance is a relative.

8ᵇ21. It is perhaps hard to make firm statements on such questions without having examined them many times. Still, to have gone through the various difficulties is not unprofitable.

CHAPTER 8

8ᵇ25. By a *quality* I mean that in virtue of which things are said to be qualified somehow. But quality is one of the things spoken of in a number of ways.

8ᵇ26. One kind of quality let us call *states* and *conditions*. A state differs from a condition in being more stable and lasting longer. Such are the branches of knowledge and the virtues. For knowledge seems to be something permanent and hard to change if one has even a moderate grasp of a branch of knowledge, unless a great change is brought about by illness or some other such thing. So also virtue; justice, temperance, and the rest seem to be not easily changed. It is what are easily changed and quickly changing that we call conditions, e.g. hotness and chill and sickness and health and the like. For a man is in a certain condition in virtue of these but he changes quickly from hot to cold and from being healthy to being sick. Similarly with the rest, unless indeed even one of these were eventually to become through length of time part of a man's nature and irremediable or exceedingly hard to change— and *then* one would perhaps call this a state. It is obvious that by 'a state' people do mean what is more lasting and harder to change. For those who lack full mastery of a branch of knowledge and are easily changed are not said to be in a state of knowledge, though they are of course in some condition, a better or a worse, in regard to that knowledge. Thus a state differs from a condition in that the one is easily changed while the other lasts longer and is harder to change.

9ᵃ10. States are also conditions but conditions are not necessarily states. For people in a state are, in virtue of this, also in some condition, but people in a condition are not in every case also in a state.

9ᵃ14. Another kind of quality is that in virtue of which we call people boxers or runners or healthy or sickly— anything, in short, which they are called in virtue of a natural capacity or incapacity. For it is not because one is in some condition that one is called anything of this sort, but because one has a natural capacity for doing something easily or for being unaffected. For example, people are called boxers or runners not because they are in some condition but because they have a natural capacity to do something easily; they are called healthy because they have a natural capacity not to be affected easily by what befalls them, and sickly because they have an incapacity to be unaffected. Similarly with the hard and the soft: the hard is so called because it has a capacity not to be divided easily, the soft because it has an incapacity for this same thing.

9ᵃ28. A third kind of quality consists of *affective qualities* and *affections*. Examples of such are sweetness, bitterness, sourness, and all their kin, and also hotness and coldness and paleness and darkness. That these are qualities is obvious, for things that possess them are said to be qualified in virtue of them. Thus honey because it possesses sweetness is called sweet, and a body pale because it possesses paleness, and similarly with the others. They are called *affective* qualities not because the things that possess them have themselves been affected somehow— for honey is not called sweet because it has been affected somehow nor is any other such thing. Similarly, hotness and coldness are not called affective qualities because the things that possess them have themselves been affected somehow, but it is because each of the qualities mentioned is productive of an affection of the senses that they are called affective qualities. For sweetness produces a certain affection of taste, hotness one of touch, and the rest likewise.

9ᵇ9. Paleness and darkness, however, and other colourings are not called affective qualities in the same way as those just mentioned, but because they themselves have been brought about by an affection. That many changes of colour do come about through an affection is clear; when ashamed one goes red, when frightened one turns pale, and so on. And so if somebody suffers by nature from some such affection it is reasonable that he should have the corresponding colouring. For the very same bodily condition which occurs now when one is ashamed might occur also in virtue of a man's natural make-up, so that the corresponding colouring too would come about by nature.

9ᵇ19. When such circumstances have their origin in affections that are hard to change and permanent they are called qualities. For if pallor or darkness have come about in the natural make-up they are called qualities (for in virtue of them we are said to be qualified); and if pallor or darkness have resulted from long illness or from sunburn, and do not easily give way—or even last for a lifetime—these too are called qualities (since, as before, in virtue of them we are said to be qualified). But those that result from something that easily disperses and quickly gives way are called affections; for people are not, in virtue of them, said to be qualified somehow. Thus a man who reddens through shame is not called ruddy, nor one who pales in fright pallid; rather he is said to have been affected somehow. Hence such things are called affections but not qualities.

9ᵇ33. Similarly with regard to the soul also we speak of affective qualities and affections. Those which are present right from birth as a result of certain affections are called qualities, for example, madness and irascibility and the like; for in virtue of these people are said to be qualified, being called mad and irascible. Similarly with any aberrations that are not natural but result from some other circumstances, and are hard to get rid of or even completely unchangeable; such things, too, are qualities, for in virtue of them people are said to be qualified. But those which result from things that quickly subside are called affections, e.g. if a man in distress is rather bad-tempered; for the man who in such an affection is rather bad-tempered is not said to be bad-tempered, but rather he is said to have been affected somehow. Hence such things are called affections but not qualities.

10ᵃ11. A fourth kind of quality is shape and the external form of each thing, and in addition straightness and curvedness and anything like these. For in virtue of each of these a thing is said to be qualified somehow; because it is a triangle or square it is said to be qualified somehow, and because it is straight or curved. And in virtue of its form each thing is said to be qualified somehow.

10ᵃ16. 'Open-textured' and 'close-textured' and 'rough' and 'smooth' might be thought to signify a qualification; they seem, however, to be foreign to the classification of qualifications. It seems rather to be a certain position of the parts that each of them reveals. For a thing is close-textured because its parts are close together, open-textured because they are separated from one another; smooth because its parts lie somehow on a straight line, rough because somé stick up above others.

10ª25. Perhaps some other manner of quality might come to light, but we have made a pretty complete list of those most spoken of.

10ª27. These, then, that we have mentioned are *qualities*, while things called paronymously because of these or called in some other way from them are *qualified*. Now in most cases, indeed in practically all, things are called paronymously, as the pale man from paleness, the grammatical from grammar, the just from justice, and so on. But in some cases, because there are no names for the qualities, it is impossible for things to be called paronymously from them. For example, the runner or the boxer, so called in virtue of a natural capacity, is not called paronymously from any quality; for there are no names for the capacities in virtue of which these men are said to be qualified—as there *are* for the branches of knowledge in virtue of which men are called boxers or wrestlers with reference to their condition (for we speak of boxing and of wrestling as branches of knowledge, and it is paronymously from them that those in the condition are said to be qualified). Sometimes, however, even when there is a name for a quality, that which is said to be qualified in virtue of it is not so called paronymously. For example, the good man is so called from virtue, since it is because he has virtue that he is called good; but he is not called paronymously from virtue. This sort of case is, however, rare. Things then that are called paronymously from the qualities we mentioned, or called from them in some other way, are said to be qualified.

10ᵇ12. There is contrariety in regard to qualification. For example, justice is contrary to injustice and whiteness to blackness, and so on; also things said to be qualified in virtue of them—the unjust to the just and the white to the black. But this is not so in all cases; for there is no contrary to red or yellow or such colours though they are qualifications.

10^{b}17. Further, if one of a pair of contraries is a qualification, the other too will be a qualification. This is clear if one examines the other predicates. For example, if justice is contrary to injustice and justice is a qualification, then injustice too is a qualification. For none of the other predicates fits injustice, neither quantity nor relative nor where nor in fact any other such predicate except qualification. Similarly with the other contraries that involve qualification.

10^{b}26. Qualifications admit of a more and a less; for one thing is called more pale or less pale than another, and more just than another. Moreover, it itself sustains increase (for what is pale can still become paler)—not in all cases though, but in most. It might be questioned whether one justice is called more a justice than another, and similarly for the other conditions. For some people dispute about such cases. They utterly deny that one justice is called more or less a justice than another, or one health more or less a health, though they say that one person has health less than another, justice less than another, and similarly with grammar and the other conditions. At any rate things spoken of in virtue of these unquestionably admit of a more and a less: one man is called more grammatical than another, juster, healthier, and so on.

11^{a}5. Triangle and square do not seem to admit of a more, nor does any other shape. For things which admit the definition of triangle or circle are all equally triangles or circles, while of things which do not admit it none will

be called *more that* than another—a square is not more
a circle than an oblong is, for neither admits the definition
of circle. In short, unless both admit the definition of
what is under discussion neither will be called more that
than the other. Thus not all qualifications admit of a more
and a less.

11ᵃ15. Nothing so far mentioned is distinctive of quality,
but it is in virtue of qualities only that things are called
similar and *dissimilar*; a thing is not similar to another in
virtue of anything but that in virtue of which it is qualified.
So it would be distinctive of quality that a thing is called
similar or dissimilar in virtue of it.

11ᵃ20. We should not be disturbed lest someone may
say that though we proposed to discuss quality we are
counting in many relatives (since states and conditions
are relatives). For in pretty well all such cases the genera
are spoken of in relation to something, but none of the particular cases is. For knowledge, a genus, is called just what
it is, of something else (it is called knowledge of something); but none of the particular cases is called just what
it is, of something else. For example, grammar is not called
grammar of something nor music music of something. If
at all it is in virtue of the genus that these too are spoken
of in relation to something: grammar is called knowledge
of something (not grammar of something) and music
knowledge of something (not music of something). Thus
the particular cases are not relatives. But it is with the
particular cases that we are said to be qualified, for it is
these which we possess (it is because we have some particular knowledge that we are called knowledgeable). Hence
these—the particular cases, in virtue of which we are on
occasion said to be qualified—would indeed be qualities;
and these are not relatives.

11^{a}37. Moreover, if the same thing really is a qualification and a relative there is nothing absurd in its being counted in both the genera.

CHAPTER 9

11^{b}1. Doing and being-affected admit of contrariety and of a more and a less. For heating is contrary to cooling, and being heated to being cooled, and being pleased to being pained; so they admit of contrariety. And of a more and a less also. For it is possible to heat more and less, and to be heated more and less, and to be pained more and less; hence doing and being-affected admit of a more and a less.

.   .   .   .

11^{b}10. [So much, then, is said about these; and about being-in-a-position too it has been remarked, in the discussion of relatives, that it is spoken of paronymously from the positions. About the rest, when and where and having, owing to their obviousness nothing further is said about them than what was said at the beginning, that having is signified by 'having-shoes-on', 'having-armour-on', where by, for example, 'in the Lyceum'—and all the other things that were said about them.]

CHAPTER 10

11^{b}15. [About the proposed genera, then, enough has been said; but something must be said about opposites and the various ways in which things are customarily opposed.]

11^{b}17. Things are said to be opposed to one another in four ways: as relatives or as contraries or as privation and possession or as affirmation and negation. Examples of things thus opposed (to give a rough idea) are: as relatives, the double and the half; as contraries, the good and the bad; as privation and possession, blindness and sight; as affirmation and negation, "he is sitting' and 'he is not sitting'.

11^{b}24. Things opposed as *relatives* are called just what they are, *of* their opposites or in some other way *in relation to* them. For example, the double is called just what it is (double) *of* the half. Again, knowledge and the knowable are opposed as relatives, and knowledge is called just what it is, *of* the knowable, and the knowable too is called just what it is, in relation to its opposite, knowledge; for the knowable is called knowable *by* something—by knowledge. Thus things opposed as relatives are called just what they are, *of* their opposites or in some other way *in relation to* one another.

11^{b}33. Things opposed as *contraries*, however, are never called just what they are, in relation to one another, though they are called *contraries of* one another. For the good is not called *good of* the bad, but the contrary of it; and the white not *white of* the black, but its contrary. Thus these oppositions differ from one another.

11^{b}38. If contraries are such that it is necessary for one or the other of them to belong to the things they naturally occur in or are predicated of, there is nothing intermediate between them. For example, sickness and health naturally occur in animals' bodies and it is indeed necessary for one or the other to belong to an animal's body, either sickness or health; again, odd and even are predicated of numbers, and it is indeed necessary for one or the other to belong to a number, either odd or even. And between these there is certainly nothing intermediate—between sickness and health or odd and even. But if it is not necessary for one or the other to belong, there is something intermediate between them. For example, black and white naturally occur in bodies, but it is not necessary for one or the other of them to belong to a body (for not every body is either white or black); again, bad and good are predicated both of men and of many other things, but it is not necessary for one or the other of them to belong to those things they are predicated of (for not all are either bad or good). And between these there is certainly something intermediate—between white and black are grey yellow and all other colours, and between the bad and the good the neither bad nor good. In some cases there exist names for the intermediates, as with grey and yellow between white and black; in some, however, it is not easy to find a name for the intermediate, but it is by the negation of each of the extremes that the intermediate is marked off, as with the neither good nor bad and neither just nor unjust.

12ª26. *Privation* and *possession* are spoken of in connexion with the same thing, for example sight and blindness in connexion with the eye. To generalize, each of them is spoken of in connexion with whatever the possession naturally occurs in. We say that anything capable of receiving a possession is deprived of it when it is entirely absent from that which naturally has it, and absent at the time when it is natural for it to have it. For it is not what has not teeth that we call toothless, or what has not sight blind, but what has not got them at the time when it is natural for it to have them. For some things from birth have neither sight nor teeth yet are not called toothless or blind.

12ª35. Being deprived and possessing are not privation and possession. For sight is a possession and blindness a privation, but having sight is not sight nor is being blind blindness. For blindness is a particular privation but being blind is being deprived, not a privation. Moreover, if blindness were the same as being blind both would be predicated of the same thing. But though a man is called blind a man is certainly not called blindness. These do, however, seem to be opposed—being deprived and having a possession—as privation and possession are. For the manner of opposition is the same. For as blindness is opposed to sight so also is being blind opposed to having sight. (Nor is what underlies an affirmation or negation itself an affirmation or negation. For an affirmation is an affirmative statement and a negation a negative statement, whereas none of the things underlying an affirmation or negation is a statement. These are, however, said to be opposed to one another as affirmation and negation are, for in these cases, too, the manner of opposition is the same. For in the way an affirmation is opposed to a negation, for example 'he is sitting'—'he is not sitting', so are opposed also the actual things underlying each, his sitting —his not sitting.)

12^{b}16. That privation and possession are not opposed as relatives is plain. For neither is called just what it is, of its opposite. Sight is not sight of blindness nor is it spoken of in any other way in relation to it; nor would one call blindness blindness of sight—blindness is called privation of sight but is not called blindness of sight. Moreover, all relatives are spoken of in relation to correlatives that reciprocate, so that with blindness, too, if it were a relative, that in relation to which it is spoken of would reciprocate; but it does not reciprocate, since sight is not called sight of blindness.

12^{b}26. Nor are cases of privation and possession opposed as contraries, as is clear from the following. With contraries between which there is nothing intermediate it is necessary for one or the other of them always to belong to the things they naturally occur in or are predicated of. For there was nothing intermediate in just those cases where it was necessary for one or the other to belong to a thing capable of receiving them, as with sickness and health and odd and even. But where there is something intermediate it is never necessary for one or the other to belong to everything; it is not necessary for everything to be white or black that is capable of receiving them, or hot or cold, since something intermediate between these may perfectly well be present. Moreover, there was something intermediate in just those cases where it was not necessary for one or the other to belong to a thing capable of receiving them—except for things to which the one belongs by nature, as being hot belongs to fire and being white to snow; and in these cases it is necessary for definitely one or the other to belong, and not as chance has it. For it is not possible for fire to be cold or snow black. Thus it is not necessary for one or the other of them to belong to everything capable of receiving them, but only to things to which the one belongs by nature, and in these cases it must be definitely the one and not as chance has it.

13^{a}3. But neither of these accounts is true of privation and possession. For it is not necessary for one or the other of them always to belong to a thing capable of receiving them, since if it is not yet natural for something to have sight it is not said either to be blind or to have sight; so that these would not be contraries of the sort that have nothing intermediate between them. Nor, however, of the sort that do have something intermediate between them. For it is necessary at some time for one or the other of them to belong to everything capable of receiving them. For when once it is natural for something to have sight

then it will be said either to be blind or to have sight—
not definitely one or the other of these but as chance has
it, since it is not necessary either for it to be blind or for
it to have sight, but as chance has it. But with contraries
which have something intermediate between them we
said it was never necessary for one or the other to belong
to everything, but to certain things, and to them definitely
the one. Hence it is clear that things opposed as privation
and possession are not opposed in either of the ways contraries are.

13ª17. Further, with contraries it is possible (while the
thing capable of receiving them is there) for change into
one another to occur, unless the one belongs to something
by nature as being hot does to fire. For it is possible for the
healthy to fall sick and for the white to become black and
the hot cold; and it is possible to become bad instead of
good or good instead of bad. (For the bad man, if led into
better ways of living and talking, would progress, if only
a little, towards being better. And if he once made even
a little progress it is clear that he might either change
completely or make really great progress. For however
slight the progress he made to begin with, he becomes ever
more easily changed towards virtue, so that he is likely to
make still more progress; and when this keeps happening
it brings him over completely into the contrary state, provided time permits.) With privation and possession, on the
other hand, it is impossible for change into one another
to occur. For change occurs from possession to privation
but from privation to possession is impossible; one who has
gone blind does not recover sight nor does a bald man
regain his hair nor does a toothless man grow new ones.

13ª37. It is plain that things opposed as affirmation and
negation are not opposed in any of the above ways, for

only with them is it necessary always for one to be true and the other one false. For with contraries it is not necessary always for one to be true and the other false, nor with relatives nor with possession and privation. For example, health and sickness are contraries, and neither is either true or false; similarly, the double and the half are opposed as relatives, and neither of them is either true or false; nor are cases of possession and privation, such as sight and blindness. Nothing, in fact, that is said without combination is either true or false; and all the above *are* said without combination.

13^{b}12. It might, indeed, very well seem that the same sort of thing does occur in the case of contraries said *with* combination, 'Socrates is well' being contrary to 'Socrates is sick'. Yet not even with these is it necessary always for one to be true and the other false. For if Socrates exists one will be true and one false, but if he does not both will be false; neither 'Socrates is sick' nor 'Socrates is well' will be true if Socrates himself does not exist at all. As for possession and privation, if he does not exist at all neither is true, while not always one or the other is true if he does. For 'Socrates has sight' is opposed to 'Socrates is blind' as possession to privation; and if he exists it is not necessary for one or the other to be true or false (since until the time when it is natural for him to have it both are false), while if Socrates does not exist at all then again both are false, both 'he has sight' and 'he is blind'. But with an affirmation and negation one will always be false and the other true whether he exists or not. For take 'Socrates is sick' and 'Socrates is not sick': if he exists it is clear that one or the other of them will be true or false, and equally if he does not; for if he does not exist 'he is sick' is false but 'he is not sick' true. Thus it would be distinctive of these alone—opposed affirmations and negations—that always one or the other of them is true or false.

13^b36. What is contrary to a good thing is necessarily bad; this is clear by induction from cases—health and sickness, justice and injustice, courage and cowardice, and so on with the rest. But what is contrary to a bad thing is sometimes good but sometimes bad. For excess is contrary to deficiency, which is bad, and is itself bad; yet moderation as well is contrary to both, and it is good. However, though this sort of thing may be seen in a few cases, in most cases what is contrary to a bad thing is always a good.

14^a6. With contraries it is not necessary if one exists for the other to exist too. For if everyone were well health would exist but not sickness, and if everything were white whiteness would exist but not blackness. Further, if Socrates's being well is contrary to Socrates's being sick, and it is not possible for both to hold at the same time of the same person, it would not be possible if one of the contraries existed for the other to exist too; if Socrates's being well existed Socrates's being sick would not.

14^a15. It is clearly the nature of contraries to belong to the same thing (the same either in species or in genus)—sickness and health in an animal's body, but whiteness and blackness in a body simply, and justice and injustice in a soul.

14^a19. All contraries must either be in the same genus or in contrary genera, or be themselves genera. For white and black are in the same genus (since colour is their genus), but justice and injustice are in contrary genera (since the genus of one is virtue, of the other vice), while good and bad are not in a genus but are themselves actually genera of certain things.

CHAPTER 12

14ᵃ26. One thing is called prior to another in four ways.
First and most strictly, in respect of time, as when one
thing is called older or more ancient than another; for it
is because the time is longer that it is called either older
or more ancient. Secondly, what does not reciprocate as
to implication of existence. For example, one is prior to
two because if there are two it follows at once that there
is one whereas if there is one there are not necessarily two,
so that the implication of the other's existence does not
hold reciprocally from one; and that from which the implication of existence does not hold reciprocally is thought
to be prior. Thirdly, a thing is called prior in respect of
some order, as with sciences and speeches. For in the
demonstrative sciences there is a prior and posterior in
order, for the elements are prior in order to the diagrams
(and in grammar the sound-elements are prior to the
syllables); likewise with speeches, for the introduction is
prior in order to the exposition. Further, besides the ways
mentioned what is better and more valued is thought to
be prior by nature; quite ordinary people are wont to say
of those they specially value and love that they 'have
priority'. This fourth way is perhaps the least proper.

14ᵇ9. There are, then, this many ways of speaking of the
prior. There would seem, however, to be another manner
of priority besides those mentioned. For of things which
reciprocate as to implication of existence, that which is
in some way the cause of the other's existence might
reasonably be called prior by nature. And that there are
some such cases is clear. For there being a man reciprocates as to implication of existence with the true statement
about it: if there is a man, the statement whereby we say
that there is a man is true, and reciprocally—since if the

statement whereby we say that there is a man is true, there is a man. And whereas the true statement is in no way the cause of the actual thing's existence, the actual thing does seem in some way the cause of the statement's being true; it is because the actual thing exists or does not that the statement is called true or false. Thus there are five ways in which one thing might be called prior to another.

CHAPTER 13

$14^{b}24$. Those things are called *simultaneous* without qualification and most strictly which come into being at the same time; for neither is prior or posterior. These are called simultaneous in respect of time. But those things are called *simultaneous by nature* which reciprocate as to implication of existence, provided that neither is in any way the cause of the other's existence, e.g. the double and the half. These reciprocate, since if there is a double there is a half and if there is a half there is a double, but neither is the cause of the other's existence. Also, co-ordinate species of the same genus are called simultaneous by nature. It is those resulting from the same division that are called co-ordinate, e.g. bird and beast and fish. For these are of the same genus and co-ordinate, since animal is divided into these—into bird and beast and fish—and none of them is prior or posterior; and things of this kind are thought to be simultaneous by nature. Each of these might itself be further divided into species (I mean beast and bird and fish); so there, too, those resulting from the same division of the same genus will be simultaneous by nature. Genera, however, are always prior to species since they do not reciprocate as to implication of existence; e.g. if there is a fish there is an animal, but if there is an animal there is not necessarily a fish. Thus we call simultaneous by nature those things which reciprocate as to implication of existence provided that neither is in any way the cause of the other's existence; and also co-ordinate species of the same genus. And we call simultaneous without qualification things which come into being at the same time.

CHAPTER 14

15ª13. There are six kinds of change: generation, destruction, increase, diminution, alteration, change of place. That the rest are distinct from one another is obvious (for generation is not destruction, nor yet is increase or diminution,[1] nor is change of place; and similarly with the others too), but there is a question about alteration— whether it is not perhaps necessary for what is altering to be altering in virtue of one of the other changes. However, this is not true. For in pretty well all the affections, or most of them, we undergo alteration without partaking of any of the other changes. For what changes as to an affection does not necessarily increase or diminish—and likewise with the others. Thus alteration would be distinct from the other changes. For if it were the same, a thing altering would, as such, have to be increasing too or diminishing, or one of the other changes would have to follow; but this is not necessary. Equally, a thing increasing—or undergoing some other change—would have to be altering. But there are things that increase without altering, as a square is increased by the addition of a gnomon but is not thereby altered; similarly, too, with other such cases. Hence the changes are distinct from one another.

15ᵇ1. Change in general is contrary to staying the same. As for the particular kinds, destruction is contrary to generation and diminution to increase, while change of place

---

[1] Read ἡ αὔξησις ⟨ἡ⟩ μείωσις.

seems most opposed to staying in the same place—and perhaps to change towards the contrary place (upward change of place, for example, being opposed to downward and downward to upward). As for the other change in our list, it is not easy to state what is contrary to it. There seems to be nothing contrary, unless here too one were to oppose staying the same in qualification or change towards the contrary qualification (just as with change of place we had staying in the same place or change towards the contrary place). For alteration is change in qualification. Thus to change in qualification is opposed staying the same in qualification or change towards the contrary qualification (becoming white, for example, being opposed to becoming black). For a thing alters through the occurrence of change towards contrary qualifications.

CHAPTER 15

15^b17. *Having* is spoken of in a number of ways: having as a state and condition or some other quality (we are said to have knowledge and virtue); or as a quantity, like the height someone may have (he is said to have a height of five feet or six feet); or as things on the body, like a cloak or tunic; or as on a part, like a ring on a hand; or as a part, like a hand or foot; or as in a container, as with the measure of wheat or the jar of wine (for the jar is said to have wine, and the measure wheat, so these are said to have as in a container); or as a possession (for we are said to have a house and a field). One is also said to have a wife, and a wife a husband, but this seems to be a very strange way of 'having', since by 'having a wife' we signify nothing other than that he is married to her. Some further ways of having might perhaps come to light, but we have made a pretty complete enumeration of those commonly spoken of.

DE INTERPRETATIONE

CHAPTER I

16ª1. First we must settle what a name is and what a verb is, and then what a negation, an affirmation, a statement and a sentence are.

16ª3. Now spoken sounds are symbols of affections in the soul, and written marks symbols of spoken sounds. And just as written marks are not the same for all men, neither are spoken sounds. But what these are in the first place signs of—affections of the soul—are the same for all; and what these affections are likenesses of—actual things—are also the same. These matters have been discussed in the work on the soul and do not belong to the present subject.

16ª9. Just as some thoughts in the soul are neither true nor false while some are necessarily one or the other, so also with spoken sounds. For falsity and truth have to do with combination and separation. Thus names and verbs by themselves—for instance 'man' or 'white' when nothing further is added—are like the thoughts that are without combination and separation; for so far they are neither true nor false. A sign of this is that even 'goat-stag' signifies something but not, as yet, anything true or false—unless 'is' or 'is not' is added (either simply or with reference to time).

CHAPTER 2

16ª19. A *name* is a spoken sound significant by convention, without time, none of whose parts is significant in separation.

16ᵃ21. For in 'Whitfield' the 'field' does not signify anything in its own right, as it does in the phrase 'white field'. Not that it is the same with complex names as with simple ones: in the latter the part is in no way significant, in the former it has some force but is not significant of anything in separation, for example the 'boat' in 'pirate-boat'.

16ᵃ26. I say 'by convention' because no name is a name naturally but only when it has become a symbol. Even inarticulate noises (of beasts, for instance) do indeed reveal something, yet none of them is a name.

16ᵃ29. 'Not man' is not a name, nor is there any correct name for it. It is neither a phrase nor a negation. Let us call it an indefinite name.

16ᵃ32. 'Philo's', 'to-Philo', and the like are not names but inflexions of names. The same account holds for them as for names except that an inflexion when combined with 'is', 'was', or 'will be' is not true or false whereas a name always is. Take, for example, 'Philo's is' or 'Philo's is not'; so far there is nothing either true or false.

CHAPTER 3

16ᵇ6. A *verb* is what additionally signifies time, no part of it being significant separately; and it is a sign of things said of something else.

16ᵇ8. It additionally signifies time: 'recovery' is a name, but 'recovers' is a verb, because it additionally signifies something's holding *now*. And it is always a sign of what holds, that is, holds of a subject.

16ᵇ11. 'Does not recover' and 'does not ail' I do not call verbs. For though they additionally signify time and always hold of something, yet there is a difference—for which there is no name. Let us call them indefinite verbs, because they hold indifferently of anything whether existent or non-existent.

16ᵇ16. Similarly, 'recovered' and 'will-recover' are not verbs but inflexions of verbs. They differ from the verb in that it additionally signifies the present time, they the time outside the present.

16ᵇ19. When uttered just by itself a verb is a name and signifies something—the speaker arrests his thought and the hearer pauses—but it does not yet signify whether it is or not. For not even[1] 'to be' or 'not to be' is a sign of the actual thing (nor if you say simply 'that which is'); for by itself it is nothing, but it additionally signifies some combination, which cannot be thought of without the components.

CHAPTER 4

16ᵇ26. A *sentence* is a significant spoken sound some part of which is significant in separation—as an expression, not as an affirmation.

16ᵇ28. I mean that 'animal', for instance, signifies something, but not that it is or is not (though it will be an affirmation or negation if something is added); the single syllables of 'animal', on the other hand, signify nothing. Nor is the 'ice' in 'mice' significant; here it is simply a spoken sound. In double words, as we said, a part does signify, but not in its own right.

16ᵇ33. Every sentence is significant (not as a tool but, as we said, by convention), but not every sentence is a statement-making sentence, but only those in which there is truth or falsity. There is not truth or falsity in all sen-

[1] Read οὐδὲ γάρ.

tences: a prayer is a sentence but is neither true nor false. The present investigation deals with the statement-making sentence; the others we can dismiss, since consideration of them belongs rather to the study of rhetoric or poetry.

CHAPTER 5

17^a8. The first single statement-making sentence is the affirmation, next is the negation. The others are single in virtue of a connective.

17^a9. Every statement-making sentence must contain a verb or an inflexion of a verb. For even the definition of man is not yet a statement-making sentence—unless 'is' or 'will be' or 'was' or something of this sort is added. (To explain why 'two-footed land animal' is one thing and not many belongs to a different inquiry; certainly it will not be one simply through being said all together.)

17^a15. A single statement-making sentence is either one that reveals a single thing or one that is single in virtue of a connective. There are more than one if more things than one are revealed or if connectives are lacking.

17^a17. (Let us call a name or a verb simply an expression, since by saying it one cannot reveal anything by one's utterance in such a way as to be making a statement, whether one is answering a question or speaking spontaneously.)

17^a20. Of these the one is a simple statement, affirming or denying something of something, the other is compounded of simple statements and is a kind of composite sentence.

17^a23. The simple statement is a significant spoken sound about whether something does or does not hold (in one of the divisions of time).

CHAPTER 6

17ª25. An *affirmation* is a statement affirming something of something, a *negation* is a statement denying something of something.

17ª26. Now it is possible to state of what does hold that it does not hold, of what does not hold that it does hold, of what does hold that it does hold, and of what does not hold that it does not hold. Similarly for times outside the present. So it must be possible to deny whatever anyone has affirmed, and to affirm whatever anyone has denied. Thus it is clear that for every affirmation there is an opposite negation, and for every negation an opposite affirmation. Let us call an affirmation and a negation which are opposite a *contradiction*. I speak of statements as opposite when they affirm and deny the same thing of the same thing—not homonymously, together with all other such conditions that we add to counter the troublesome objections of sophists.

CHAPTER 7

17ª38. Now of actual things some are universal, others particular (I call universal that which is by its nature predi-cated of a number of things, and particular that which is not; man, for instance, is a universal, Callias a parti-cular). So it must sometimes be of a universal that one states that something holds or does not, sometimes of a particular. Now if one states universally of a universal that something holds or does not, there will be contrary state-ments (examples of what I mean by 'stating universally of a universal' are 'every man is white' and 'no man is white'). But when one states something of a universal but not universally, the statements are not contrary (though what is being revealed may be contrary). Examples of what I mean by 'stating of a universal not universally' are 'a man is white' and 'a man is not white'; man is a universal but it is not used universally in the statement (for 'every' does not signify the universal but that it is taken universally). It is not true to predicate a universal universally of a subject, for there cannot be an affirmation in which a universal is predicated universally of a subject, for instance 'every man is every animal'.

17ᵇ16. I call an affirmation and a negation *contradictory* opposites when what one signifies universally the other signifies not universally,[1] e.g. 'every man is white' and 'not every man is white', 'no man is white' and 'some man is white'. But I call the universal affirmation and the universal negation contrary opposites, e.g. 'every man is just' and 'no man is just'. So these cannot be true together, but their opposites may both be true with respect to the same thing, e.g. 'not every man is white' and 'some man is white'.

17ᵇ26. Of contradictory statements about a universal taken universally it is necessary for one or the other to be true or false; similarly if they are about particulars, e.g. 'Socrates is white' and 'Socrates is not white'. But if they are about a universal not taken universally it is not always the case that one is true and the other false. For it is true to say at the same time that a man is white and that a man is not white, or that a man is noble and a man is not noble (for if base, then not noble; and if something is becoming something, then it *is* not that thing). This might seem absurd at first sight, because 'a man is not white' looks as if it signifies also at the same time that no man is white; this, however, does not signify the same, nor does it necessarily hold at the same time.

---

[1] The text looks corrupt, but this is evidently the meaning.

17^{b}37. It is evident that a single affirmation has a single negation. For the negation must deny the same thing as the affirmation affirmed, and of the same thing, whether a particular or a universal (taken either universally or not universally). I mean, for example, 'Socrates is white' and 'Socrates is not white'. But if something else is denied, or the same thing is denied of something else, that will not be the opposite statement, but a different one. The opposite of 'every man is white' is 'not every man is white'; of 'some man is white', 'no man is white'; of 'a man is white', 'a man is not white'.

18^{a}8. We have explained, then: that a single affirmation has a single negation as its contradictory opposite, and which these are; that contrary statements are different, and which these are; and that not all contradictory pairs are true or false, why this is, and when they are true or false.

CHAPTER 8

18^{a}13. A single affirmation or negation is one which signifies one thing about one thing (whether about a universal taken universally or not), e.g. 'every man is white', 'not every man is white', 'a man is white', 'a man is not white', 'no man is white', 'some man is white'—assuming that 'white' signifies one thing.

18^{a}18. But if one name is given to two things which do not make up one thing, there is not a single affirmation. Suppose, for example, that one gave the name 'cloak' to horse and man; 'a cloak is white' would not be a single affirmation. For to say this is no different from saying 'a horse and a man is white', and this is no different from saying 'a horse is white and a man is white'. So if this last signifies more than one thing and is more than one affirmation, clearly the first also signifies either more than one thing or nothing (because no man is a horse). Consequently it is not necessary, with these statements either, for one contradictory to be true and the other false.

CHAPTER 9

18ª28. With regard to what is and what has been it is necessary for the affirmation or the negation to be true or false. And with universals taken universally it is always necessary for one to be true and the other false, and with particulars too, as we have said; but with universals not spoken of universally it is not necessary. But with particulars that are going to be it is different.

18ª34. For if every affirmation or negation is true or false it is necessary for everything either to be the case or not to be the case. For if one person says that something will be and another denies this same thing, it is clearly necessary for one of them to be saying what is true—if every affirmation is true or false; for both will not be the case together under such circumstances. For if it is true to say that it is white or is not white, it is necessary for it to be white or not white; and if it is white or is not white, then it was true to say or deny this. If it is not the case it is false, if it is false it is not the case. So it is necessary for the affirmation or the negation to be true. It follows that nothing either is or is happening, or will be or will not be, by chance or as chance has it, but everything of necessity and not as chance has it (since either he who says or he who denies is saying what is true). For otherwise it might equally well happen or not happen, since what is as chance has it is no more thus than not thus, nor will it be.

18ᵇ9. Again, if it is white now it was true to say earlier that it would be white; so that it was always true to say of anything that has happened that it would be so. But if it was always true to say that it was so, or would be so, it could not not be so, or not be going to be so. But if something cannot not happen it is impossible for it not to happen; and if it is impossible for something not to happen it is necessary for it to happen. Everything that will be, therefore, happens necessarily. So nothing will come about as chance has it or by chance; for if by chance, not of necessity.

18ᵇ17. Nor, however, can we say that neither is true— that it neither will be nor will not be so. For, firstly, though the affirmation is false the negation is not true, and though the negation is false the affirmation, on this view, is not true. Moreover, if it is true to say that something is white and large[1], both have to hold of it, and if true that they will hold tomorrow, they will have to hold tomorrow[2]; and if it neither will be nor will not be the case tomorrow, then there is no 'as chance has it'. Take a sea-battle: it would *have* neither to happen nor not to happen.

18ᵇ26. These and others like them are the absurdities that follow if it is necessary, for every affirmation and negation either about universals spoken of universally or about particulars, that one of the opposites be true and the other false, and that nothing of what happens is as chance has it, but everything is and happens of necessity. So there would be no need to deliberate or to take trouble (thinking that if we do this, this will happen, but if we do not, it will not). For there is nothing to prevent someone's having said ten thousand years beforehand that this would be the case, and another's having denied it; so that whichever of the two was true to say then, will be the case of necessity. Nor, of course, does it make any difference whether any people made the contradictory statements

---

[1] Read λευκὸν καὶ μέγα.
[2] Read εἰ δὲ ὑπάρξει . . ., ὑπάρξειν . . .

or not. For clearly this is how the actual things are even
if someone did not affirm it and another deny it. For it is
not because of the affirming or denying that it will be or
will not be the case, nor is it a question of ten thousand
years beforehand rather than any other time. Hence, if
in the whole of time the state of things was such that one
or the other was true, it was necessary for this to happen,
and for the state of things always to be such that everything that happens happens of necessity. For what anyone
has truly said would be the case cannot not happen; and
of what happens it was always true to say that it would be
the case.

19ᵃ7. But what if this is impossible? For we see that
what will be has an origin both in deliberation and in
action, and that, in general, in things that are not always
actual there is the possibility of being and of not being;
here both possibilities are open, both being and not being,
and, consequently, both coming to be and not coming to
be. Many things are obviously like this. For example, it
is possible for this cloak to be cut up, and yet it will not
be cut up but will wear out first. But equally, its not being
cut up is also possible, for it would not be the case that it
wore out first unless its not being cut up were possible. So
it is the same with all other events that are spoken of in
terms of this kind of possibility. Clearly, therefore, not
everything is or happens of necessity: some things happen
as chance has it, and of the affirmation and the negation
neither is true rather than the other; with other things it
is one rather than the other and as a rule, but still it is
possible for the other to happen instead.

19ᵃ23. What is, necessarily is, when it is; and what is not,
necessarily is not, when it is not. But not everything that
is, necessarily is; and not everything that is not, necessarily

is not. For to say that everything that is, is of necessity, when it is, is not the same as saying unconditionally that it is of necessity. Similarly with what is not. And the same account holds for contradictories: everything necessarily is or is not, and will be or will not be; but one cannot divide and say that one or the other is necessary. I mean, for example: it is necessary for there to be or not to be a sea-battle tomorrow; but it is not necessary for a sea-battle to take place tomorrow, nor for one not to take place—though it is necessary for one to take place or not to take place. So, since statements are true according to how the actual things are, it is clear that wherever these are such as to allow of contraries as chance has it, the same necessarily holds for the contradictories also. This happens with things that are not always so or are not always not so. With these it is necessary for one or the other of the contradictories to be true or false—not, however, this one or that one, but as chance has it; or for one to be true *rather* than the other, yet not *already* true or false.

19ᵃ39. Clearly, then, it is not necessary that of every affirmation and opposite negation one should be true and the other false. For what holds for things that are does not hold for things that are not but may possibly be or not be; with these it is as we have said.

CHAPTER 10

19ᵇ5. Now an affirmation signifies something about something, this last being either a name or a 'non-name'; and what is affirmed must be one thing about one thing. (Names and 'non-names' have already been discussed. For I do not call 'not-man' a name but an indefinite name— for what it signifies is in a way one thing, but indefinite— just as I do not call 'does not recover' a verb.) So every affirmation will contain either a name and a verb or an indefinite name and a verb. Without a verb there will be no affirmation or negation. 'Is', 'will be', 'was', 'becomes', and the like are verbs according to what we laid down, since they additionally signify time. So a first affirmation and negation are: 'a man is', 'a man is not'; then, 'a not-man is', 'a not-man is not'; and again, 'every man is', 'every man is not', 'every not-man is', 'every not-man is not'. For times other than the present the same account holds.

19^{b}19. But when 'is' is predicated additionally as a third thing, there are two ways of expressing opposition. (I mean, for example, 'a man is just'; here I say that the 'is' is a third component—whether name or verb—in the affirmation.) Because of this there will here be *four* cases (two of which will be related, as to order of sequence, to the affirmation and negation in the way the privations are, while two will not). I mean that 'is' will be added either to 'just' or to 'not-just', and so, too, will the negation. Thus there will be four cases. What is meant should be clear from the following diagram:

(*a*) 'a man is just'	(*b*) 'a man is not just'
	This is the negation of (*a*).
(*d*) 'a man is not not-just	(*c*) 'a man is not-just'
This is the negation of (*c*).	

'Is' and 'is not' are here added to 'just' and to 'not-just'.

19^{b}30. This then is how these are arranged (as is said in the *Analytics*). Similarly, too, if the affirmation is about the name taken universally, e.g.:

(*a*) 'every man is just'   (*b*) 'not every man is just'
(*d*) 'not every man is   (*c*) 'every man is not-just'
    not-just'

Here, however, it is not in the same way possible for diagonal statements to be true together, though it is possible sometimes.

19^b36. These, then, are two pairs of opposites. There are others if something is added to 'not-man' as a sort of subject, thus:

(*a*) 'a not-man is just'   (*b*) 'a not-man is not just'
(*d*) 'a not-man is not   (*c*) 'a not-man is not-just'
    not-just'

There will not be any more oppositions than these. These last are a group on their own separate from the others, in that they use 'not-man' as a name.

20^a3. In cases where 'is' does not fit (e.g. with 'recovers' or 'walks') the verbs have the same effect when so placed as if 'is' were joined on, e.g.:

(*a*) 'every man walks'   (*b*) 'every man does not walk'
(*d*) 'every not-man does (*c*) 'every not-man walks'
    not walk'

Here one must not say 'not every man' but must add the 'not', the negation, to 'man'. For 'every' does not signify a universal, but that it is taken universally. This is clear from the following:

(*a*) 'a man walks'   (*b*) 'a man does not walk'
(*d*) 'a not-man does (*c*) 'a not-man walks'
    not walk'

For these differ from the previous ones in not being universal. So 'every' or 'no' additionally signify nothing other than that the affirmation or negation is about the name taken universally. Everything else, therefore, must be added unchanged.

20ª16. Since the contrary negation of 'every animal is just' is that which signifies that no animal is just, obviously these will never be true together or of the same thing, but their opposites sometimes will (e.g. 'not every animal is just' and 'some animal is just'). 'No man is just' follows from 'every man is not-just', while the opposite of this, 'not every man is not-just', follows from 'some man is just' (for there must be one). It is clear too that, with regard to particulars, if it is true, when asked something, to deny it, it is true also to affirm something. For instance: 'Is Socrates wise? No. Then Socrates is not-wise.' With universals, on the other hand, the corresponding affirmation is not true, but the negation is true. For instance: 'Is every man wise? No. Then every man is not-wise.' This is false, but 'then not every man is wise' is true; this is the opposite statement, the other is the contrary.

20ª31. Names and verbs that are indefinite (and thereby opposite), such as 'not-man' and 'not-just', might be thought to be negations without a name and a verb. But they are not. For a negation must always be true or false; but one who says 'not-man'—without adding anything else—has no more said something true or false (indeed rather less so) than one who says 'man'.

20ª37. 'Every not-man is just' does not signify the same as any of the above, nor does its opposite, 'not every not-man is just'. But 'every not-man is not-just' signifies the same as 'no not-man is just'.

20ᵇ1. If names and verbs are transposed they still signify the same thing, e.g. 'a man is white' and 'white is a man'.

For otherwise the same statement will have more than one negation, whereas we have shown that one has only one. For 'a man is white' has for negation 'a man is not white', while 'white is a man'—if it is not the same as 'a man is white'—will have for negation either 'white is not a not-man' or 'white is not a man'. But one of these is a negation of 'white is a not-man', the other of 'a man is white'. Thus there will be two negations of one statement. Clearly, then, if the name and the verb are transposed the same affirmation and negation are produced.

CHAPTER 11

20^{b}12. To affirm or deny one thing of many, or many of one, is not *one* affirmation or negation unless the many things together make up some one thing. I do not call them one if there exists one name but there is not some one thing they make up. For example, man is perhaps an animal and two-footed and tame, yet these do make up some one thing; whereas white and man and walking do not make up one thing. So if someone affirms some one thing of these it is not one affirmation; it is one spoken sound, but more than one affirmation. Similarly, if these are affirmed of one thing, that is more than one affirmation. So if a dialectical question demands as answer either the statement proposed or one side of a contradiction (the statement in fact being a side of one contradiction), there could not be *one* answer in these cases. For the question itself would not be one question, even if true. These matters have been discussed in the *Topics*. (It is also clear that 'What is it?' is not a dialectical question either; for the question must give one the choice of stating whichever side of the contradiction one wishes. The questioner must specify further and ask whether man is this or not this.)

20ᵇ31. Of things predicated separately some can be predicated in combination, the whole predicate as one, others cannot. What then is the difference? For of a man it is true to say two-footed separately and animal separately, and also to say them as one; similarly, white and man separately, and also as one. But if someone is good and a cobbler it does not follow that he is a good cobbler. For if because each of two holds both together also hold, there will be many absurdities. For since of a man both 'white' and 'a man' are true, so also is the whole compound; again, if 'white' then the whole compound—so that he will be a white white man, and so on indefinitely. Or, again, we shall have 'walking white musician', and then these compounded many times over. Further, if Socrates is a man and is Socrates he will be a man Socrates; and if two-footed and a man then a two-footed man. Clearly, then, one is led into many absurdities if one lays down without restriction that the compounds come about. How the matter should be put we will now explain.

21ᵃ7. Of things predicated, and things they get predicated of, those which are said accidentally, either of the same thing or of one another, will not be one. For example, a man is white and musical, but 'white' and 'musical' are not one, because they are both accidental to the same thing. And even if it is true to say that the white is musical, 'musical white' will still not be one thing; for it is accidentally that the musical is white, and so 'white musical' will not be one[1]. Nor, consequently, will the cobbler who is (without qualification) good, though an animal which is two-footed will (since this is not accidental). Further, where one of the things is contained in the other, they will not be one. This is why 'white' is not repeated and why a man is not an animal man or a two-footed

---

[1] Read μουσικὸν ἕν.

man; for two-footed and animal are contained in man.

21ᵃ18. It is true to speak of the particular case even
without qualification; e.g. to say that some particular man
is a man or some particular white man white. Not always,
though. When in what is added some opposite is contained
from which a contradiction follows, it is not true but false
(e.g. to call a dead man a man); but when no such opposite is contained, it is true. Or rather, when it is contained
it is always not true, but when it is not, it is not always
true. For example, Homer is something (say, a poet). Does
it follow that he is? No, for the 'is' is predicated accidentally of Homer; for it is because he is a poet, not in its own
right, that the 'is' is predicated of Homer. Thus, where
predicates *both* contain no contrariety if definitions are put
instead of names *and* are predicated in their own right and
not accidentally, in these cases it will be true to speak of
the particular thing even without qualification. It is not
true to say that what is not, since it is thought about, is
something that is; for what is thought about it is not that
it is, but that it is not.

CHAPTER 12

21ᵃ34. Having cleared up these points, we must consider how negations and affirmations of the possible to
be and the not possible are related to one another, and
of the admissible and not admissible, and about the
impossible and the necessary. For there are some puzzles
here.

21ᵃ38. Suppose we say that of combined expressions
those are the contradictory opposites of one another which
are ordered by reference to 'to be' and 'not to be'. For
example, the negation of 'to be a man' is 'not to be a
man', not 'to be a not-man', and the negation of 'to be

a white man' is 'not to be a white man', not 'to be a not-white man' (otherwise, since of everything the affirmation or the negation holds, the log will be truly said *to be a not-white man*). And if this is so, in cases where 'to be' is not added what is said instead of 'to be' will have the same effect. For example, the negation of 'a man walks' is not 'a not-man walks' but 'a man does not walk'; for there is no difference between saying that a man walks and saying that a man is walking. So then, if this holds good everywhere, the negation of 'possible to be' is 'possible not to be', and not 'not possible to be'. Yet it seems that for the same thing it is possible both to be and not to be. For everything capable of being cut or of walking is capable also of not walking or of not being cut. The reason is that whatever is capable in this way is not always actual, so that the negation too will hold of it: what can walk is capable also of not walking, and what can be seen of not being seen. But it is impossible for opposite expressions to be true of the same thing. This then is not the negation. For it follows from the above that either the same thing is said and denied of the same thing at the same time, or it is not by 'to be' and 'not to be' being added that affirmations and negations are produced. So if the former is impossible we must choose the latter. The negation of 'possible to be', therefore, is 'not possible to be'. The same account holds for 'admissible to be': its negation is 'not admissible to be'. Similarly with the others, 'necessary' and 'impossible'. For as in the previous examples 'to be' and 'not to be' are additions, while the actual things that are subjects are white and man, so here 'to be' serves as subject, while 'to be possible' and 'to be admissible' are additions—these determining the possible and not possible in the case of 'to be', just as in the previous cases 'to be' and 'not to be' determine the true.

21^{b}34. The negation of 'possible not to be' is 'not possible not to be'. This is why 'possible to be' and 'possible not to be' may be thought actually to follow from one another. For it is possible for the same thing to be and not to be; such statements are not contradictories of one another. But 'possible to be' and 'not possible to be' never hold together, because they are opposites. Nor do 'possible not to be' and 'not possible not to be' ever hold together. Similarly, the negation of 'necessary to be' is not 'necessary not to be' but 'not necessary to be'; and of 'necessary not to be', 'not necessary not to be'. And of 'impossible to be' it is not 'impossible not to be' but 'not impossible to be'; and of 'impossible not to be', 'not impossible not to be'. Universally, indeed, as has been said, one must treat 'to be' and 'not to be' as the subjects, and these others must be joined on to 'to be' and 'not to be' to make affirmations and negations. We must take the opposite expressions to be these: 'possible'—'not possible'; 'admissible'—'not admissible'; 'impossible'—'not impossible'; 'necessary'—'not necessary'; 'true'—'not true'.

CHAPTER 13

22^{a}14. With this treatment the implications work out in a reasonable way. From 'possible to be' follow 'admissible to be' (and, reciprocally, the former from the latter) and 'not impossible to be' and 'not necessary to be'. From 'possible not to be' and 'admissible not to be' follow both 'not necessary not to be' and 'not impossible not to be'. From 'not possible to be' and 'not admissible to be' follow 'necessary not to be' and 'impossible to be'. From 'not possible not to be' and 'not admissible not to be' follow 'necessary to be' and 'impossible not to be'. What we are saying can be seen from the following table.

I	II
possible to be	not possible to be
admissible to be	not admissible to be
not impossible to be	impossible to be
not necessary to be	necessary not to be

III	IV
possible not to be	not possible not to be
admissible not to be	not admissible not to be
not impossible not to be	impossible not to be
not necessary not to be	necessary to be

22ᵃ32. 'Impossible' and 'not impossible' follow from 'admissible' and 'possible' and 'not possible' and 'not admissible' contradictorily but conversely: for the negation of 'impossible' follows from 'possible to be', and the affirmation from the negation, 'impossible to be' from 'not possible to be' (for 'impossible to be' is an affirmation, 'not impossible' a negation).

22ᵃ38. But what about the necessary? Evidently things are different here: it is contraries which follow, and the contradictories are separated. For the negation of 'necessary not to be' is not 'not necessary to be'. For both may be true of the same thing, since the necessary not to be is not necessary to be. The reason why these do not follow in the same way as the others is that it is when applied in a contrary way that 'impossible' and 'necessary' have the same force. For if it is impossible *to be* it is necessary for this (not, *to be*, but) *not to be*; and if it is impossible not to be it is necessary for this to be. Thus if those follow from 'possible' and 'not possible' in the same way, these follow in a contrary way, since 'necessary' and 'impossible' do signify the same but (as we said) when applied conversely.

22ᵇ10. But perhaps it is impossible for the contradictories in the case of the necessary to be placed thus? For
the necessary to be is possible to be. (Otherwise the negation will follow, since it is necessary either to affirm or to
deny it; and then, if it is not possible to be, it is impossible
to be; so the necessary to be is impossible to be—which
is absurd.) However, from 'possible to be' follows 'not
impossible to be', and from this follows 'not necessary to
be'; with the result that the necessary to be is not necessary
to be—which is absurd. However, it is not 'necessary to
be' nor yet 'necessary not to be' that follows from 'possible
to be'. For with this both may happen, but whichever of
the others is true these will no longer be true; for it is at
the same time possible to be and not to be, but if it is
necessary to be or not to be it will not be possible for both.
It remains, therefore, for 'not necessary not to be' to
follow from 'possible to be'; for this is true of 'necessary
to be' also. Moreover, this proves to be contradictory to
what follows from 'not possible to be', since from that
follow 'impossible to be' and 'necessary not to be', whose
negation is 'not necessary not to be'. So these contradictories, too, follow in the way stated, and nothing impossible
results when they are so placed.

22ᵇ29. One might raise the question whether 'possible
to be' follows from 'necessary to be'. For if it does not
follow the contradictory will follow, 'not possible to be'—
or if one were to deny that this is the contradictory one
must say that 'possible not to be' is; both of which are
false of 'necessary to be'. On the other hand, the same
thing seems to be capable of being cut and of not being
cut, of being and of not being, so that the necessary to be
will be admissible not to be; but this is false. Well now,
it is evident that not everything capable either of being or

of walking is capable of the opposites also. There are cases of which this is not true. Firstly, with things capable non-rationally; fire, for example, can heat and has an irrational capability. While the same rational capabilities are capabilities for more than one thing, for contraries, not all irrational capabilities are like this. Fire, as has been said, is not capable of heating and of not heating, and similarly with everything else that is actualized all the time. Some, indeed, even of the things with irrational capabilities are at the same time capable of opposites. But the point of our remarks is that not every capability is for opposites—not even all those which are 'capabilities' of the same kind. Again, some capabilities are homonymous. For the capable is spoken of in more than one way: either because it is true as being actualized (e.g. it is capable of walking because it walks, and in general capable of being because what is called capable already exists in actuality), or because it might be actualized (e.g. it is capable of walking because it might walk). This latter capability applies to changeable things only, the former to unchangeable things also. (Of both it is true to say that it is not impossible for them to walk, or to be—both what is already walking and actualized and what can walk.) Thus it is not true to assert the second kind of capability of that which is without qualification necessary, but it is true to assert the other. So, since the universal follows from the particular, from being of necessity there follows capability of being— though not every sort. Perhaps, indeed, the necessary and not necessary are first principles of everything's either being or not being, and one should look at the others as following from these.

23^{a}21. It is clear from what has been said that what is of necessity is in actuality; so that, if the things which always are are prior, then also actuality is prior to capability. Some things are actualities without capability (like the primary substances), others with capability (and these are prior by nature but posterior in time to the capability); and others are never actualities but only capabilities.

CHAPTER 14

23ᵃ27. Is the affirmation contrary to the negation, or the affirmation to the affirmation—the statement that every man is just contrary to the statement 'no man is just', or 'every man is just' contrary to 'every man is unjust'? Take, for example, 'Callias is just', 'Callias is not just', 'Callias is unjust'; which of these are contraries?

23ᵃ32. Now if spoken sounds follow things in the mind, and there it is the belief *of* the contrary which is contrary (e.g. the belief that every man is just is contrary to the belief 'every man is unjust'), the same must hold also of spoken affirmations. But if it is not the case there that the belief of the contrary is contrary, neither will the affirmation be contrary to the affirmation, but rather the above-mentioned negation. So we must inquire what sort of true belief is contrary to a false belief, the belief of the negation or the belief that the contrary holds. What I mean is this: there is a true belief about the good, that it is good, another (false) one, that it is not good, and yet another, that it is bad; now which of these is contrary to the true one? And if they are one belief, by reason of which is it contrary? (It is false to suppose that contrary beliefs are distinguished by being of contraries. For the belief about the good, that it is good, and the one about the bad, that it is bad, are perhaps the same—and true, whether one belief or more than one. Yet these are contrary things. It is not, then, through being of contraries that beliefs are contrary, but rather through being to the contrary effect.)

23^{b}7. Now about the good there is the belief that it is good, the belief that it is not good, and the belief that it is something else, something which does not and cannot hold of it. (We must not take any of the other beliefs, either to the effect that what does not hold holds or to the effect that what holds does not hold—for there is an indefinite number of both kinds, both of those to the effect that what does not hold holds and of those to the effect that what holds does not hold—but only those in which there is deception. And these 'are' from things from which comings-into-being arise. But comings-into-being are from opposites. So also, then, are cases of deceit.) Now the good is both good and not bad, the one in itself, the other accidentally (for it is accidental to it to be not bad); but the more true belief about anything is the one about what it is in itself; and if this holds for the true it holds also for the false. Therefore the belief that the good is not good is a false belief about what holds in itself, while the belief that it is bad is a false belief about what holds accidentally, so that the more false belief about the good would be that of the negation rather than that of the contrary. But it is he who holds the contrary belief who is most deceived with regard to anything, since contraries are among things which differ most with regard to the same thing. If, therefore, one of these is contrary, and the belief of the contradiction is *more* contrary, clearly this must be *the* contrary. The belief that the good is bad is complex, for the same person must perhaps suppose also that it is not good.

23^{b}27. Further, if in other cases also the same must hold, it would seem that we have given the correct account of this one as well. For either everywhere that of the contradiction is the contrary, or nowhere. But in cases where there *are* no contraries there is still a false belief, the one opposite to the true one; e.g. he who thinks that the man is not a man is deceived. If, therefore, these are contraries, so too elsewhere are the beliefs of the contradiction.

23^{b}33. Further, the belief about the good that it is good and that about the not good that it is not good are alike; and so, too, are the belief about the good that it is not good and that about the not good that it is good. What belief then is contrary to the true belief about the not good that it is not good? Certainly not the one which says that it is bad, for this might sometimes be true at the same time, while a true belief is never contrary to a true one. (There is something not good which is bad, so that it is possible for both to be true at the same time.) Nor again is it the belief that it is not bad, for these also might hold at the same time. There remains, then, as contrary to the belief about the not good that it is not good, the belief about the not good that it is good. Hence, too, the belief about the good that it is not good is contrary to that about the good that it is good.

24^{a}3. Evidently it will make no difference even if we make the affirmation universally. For the universal negation will be contrary; e.g. the belief that none of the goods is good will be contrary to the belief to the effect that every good is good. For if in the belief about the good that it is good 'the good' is taken universally, it is the same as the belief that whatever is good is good. And this is no different from the belief that everything which is good is good. And similarly also in the case of the not good.

24^{b}1. If then this is how it is with beliefs, and spoken affirmations and negations are symbols of things in the soul, clearly it is the universal negation about the same thing that is *contrary* to an affirmation; e.g. the contrary of 'every good is good' or 'every man is good' is 'no good is good' or 'no man is good', while 'not every good is good' or 'not every man is good' are opposed *contradictorily*. Evidently also it is not possible for either a true belief or a true contradictory statement to be contrary to a true one. For contraries are those which enclose their opposites; and while these latter may possibly be said truly by the same person, it is not possible for contraries to hold of the same thing at the same time.

NOTES

INTRODUCTORY NOTE

1. In the traditional ordering of Aristotle's works the logical treatises (the *Organon*) come first. Among the logical treatises the *Categories* and *De Interpretatione* come first, followed by the *Analytics*. This is because the *Categories* deals with terms, the constituents of propositions, the *De Interpretatione* deals with propositions, the constituents of syllogisms, and the *Analytics* deals with syllogisms.

This traditional ordering is systematic, and is therefore not a guide to the actual chronology of the writings. It is, however, probable that the *Categories* and *De Interpretatione* are in fact early works of Aristotle.

Besides being of philosophical interest in their own right, these little treatises are of peculiar importance for the history of philosophy. For they were very closely studied and much discussed both in antiquity and in the Middle Ages. They were available (if only in Latin translation) during several centuries when little else of Aristotle's work was known.

2. The *Categories* divides into three parts. Chapters 1–3 make certain preliminary points and explanations. Chapters 4–9 treat of the doctrine of categories and discuss some categories at length. Chapters 10–15 deal with a variety of topics, such as opposites, priority, and change.

The second part fades out in Chapter 9, and the passage serving as a transition to the third part (11ᵇ10–16) is certainly not genuine Aristotle. The third part itself (the *Postpraedicamenta*) has only a loose connexion with what precedes. There is no reason to doubt its authenticity, but probably it was not a part of the original *Categories* but was tacked on by an editor.

The concept of categories plays an important part in many of Aristotle's works, specially the *Metaphysics*. But it undergoes developments and refinements as Aristotle's thought develops. So the study of the *Categories* is only a first step in an investigation of Aristotle's ideas about categories.

3. The first five chapters of the *De Interpretatione* introduce and seek to define the terms 'name', 'verb', 'sentence', 'statement', 'affirmation', and 'negation'. The main body of the work (Chapters 6–11) treats of various sorts of statement, and of some of their logical properties and relationships. Chapters 12–13 are concerned with modal statements. Chapter 14 discusses a special problem about contrariety.

It is probable that Chapter 14 was originally an independent essay or lecture. The passage 23ª21–26, if by Aristotle at all, is also a later addition to the original treatise. The unhelpful title of the work (like the title of the *Categories*) is not due to Aristotle, and so need not be discussed.

The topics handled in the *De Interpretatione* recur in many other Aristotelian treatises, but particularly in the *Prior Analytics*.

CATEGORIES

1^a1. The word translated 'animal' originally meant just that; but it had come to be used also of pictures or other artistic representations (whether representations of animals or not).

The terms 'homonymous' and 'synonymous', as defined by Aristotle in this chapter, apply not to words but to things. Roughly, two things are homonymous if the same name applies to both but not in the same sense, synonymous if the same name applies to both in the same sense. Thus two things may be both homonymous and synonymous—if there is one name that applies to both but not in the same sense and another name that applies to both in the same sense. From Aristotle's distinction between 'homonymous' and 'synonymous' one could evidently derive a distinction between equivocal and unequivocal *names*; but it is important to recognize from the start that the *Categories* is not primarily or explicitly about names, but about the things that names signify. (It will be necessary in the translation and notes to use the word 'things' as a blanket-term for items in any category. It often represents the neuter plural of a Greek article, pronoun, &c.) Aristotle relies greatly on linguistic facts and tests, but his aim is to discover truths about non-linguistic items. It is incumbent on the translator not to conceal this, and, in particular, not to give a misleadingly linguistic appearance to Aristotle's statements by gratuitously supplying inverted commas in all the places where *we* might feel that it is linguistic expressions that are under discussion.

The contrast between synonyms and homonyms, between same definition and different definition, is obviously very crude. Elsewhere Aristotle recognizes that the different meanings of a word may be closely related. Thus at the beginning of *Metaphysics* Γ 2 he points out that though the force of 'healthy' varies it always has a reference to health: a healthy person is one who enjoys health, a healthy diet one which promotes health, a healthy complexion one which indicates health. Similarly, he says, with 'being': it is used in different ways when used of things in different categories, but there is a primary sense (the sense in which *substances* have being) to which all the others are related. Though the *Categories* gives emphatic priority to the category of substance it does not develop any such theory about the systematic ambiguity of 'being' or 'exists'. Chapter 1 makes it seem unlikely that Aristotle had yet seen the importance of distinguishing between words that are straightforwardly ambiguous and words whose various senses form a family or have a common nucleus. (See Aristotle's suggestions about 'good' at *Nicomachean Ethics* 1096^{b}26–28.)

1^{a}12. 'Paronymous' is obviously not a term co-ordinate with 'homo-nymous' and 'synonymous', though like them it is applied by Aristotle to things, not names. A thing is paronymous if its name is in a certain way derivative. The derivativeness in question is not etymological. Aristotle is not claiming that the word 'brave' was invented after the word 'bravery'. He is claiming rather that 'brave' *means* 'having bravery'; the brave is so called because of ('from') the bravery he has. For an X to be paronymous requires both that an X is called X because of something (feature, property, &c.) which it has (or which somehow belongs to it), and that 'X' is identical with the name of that some-thing except in ending. To say that an X gets its name from something (or is called X from something) does not necessarily imply that there is a name for the something (10^{a}32–^{b}2), or that, if there is, 'X' has any similarity to that name (10^{b}5–9). But only if these conditions are ful-filled does an X get its name from something *paronymously*.

Paronymy is commonly involved when items in categories other than substance are ascribed to substances. If we say that generosity is a virtue or that giving one's time is a (kind of) generosity, we use the name 'generosity'; but if we wish to ascribe generosity to Callias we do not say that he is generosity, but that he is generous—using a word identical except in ending with the name of the quality we are ascribing. Sometimes, indeed, the name of an item in a category is itself used to indicate the inherence of that item in a substance. In 'white is a colour' 'white' names a quality; in 'Callias is white' 'white' indicates the inherence of the quality in Callias. Here we get homon-ymy or something like it, since the definition of 'white' in the former sentence cannot be substituted for 'white' in the latter: Callias is not a colour of a certain kind (2^{a}29–34, 3^{a}15–17). There are also the possi-bilities mentioned above: an adjective indicating the inherence of something in a substance may have no similarity (or not the right kind of similarity) to the name of the something, or there may be no name for the something. So the ascription of qualities, &c., to substances does not always involve paronymy; but it very often does.

The whole idea of an X's being called X *from something* (whether paronymously or not) is of importance in the *Categories*. The categories classify things, not words. The category of quality does not include the words 'generosity' and 'generous'; nor does it include two things corresponding to the two words. It includes generosity. 'Generosity' and 'generous' introduce the very same thing, generosity, though in different ways, 'generosity' simply naming it and 'generous' serving to predicate it. Aristotle will frequently be found using or discussing distinctly predicative expressions like 'generous', because though they are not themselves names of items in categories they serve to introduce such items (e.g. the item whose name is 'generosity'). The person called generous is so called *from* generosity.

CHAPTER 2

1^{a}16. What does Aristotle mean here by 'combination' (literally, 'inter-weaving')? The word is used by Plato in the *Sophist* 262, where he makes the point that a sentence is not just a list of names or a list of verbs, but results from the combination of a name with a verb; this line of thought is taken up in the *De Interpretatione* (16^{a}9-18, 17^{a}17-20). In the present passage Aristotle's examples of expressions involving combination are both indicative sentences, and his examples of expressions without combination are all single words. Yet he ought not to intend only indicative sentences (or only sentences) to count as expressions involving combination. For in Chapter 4 he says that every expression without combination signifies an item in some one category; this implies that an expression like 'white man' which introduces two items from two categories is an expression involving combination. Nor should he mean that all and only single words are expressions lacking combination. For he treats 'in the Lyceum' and 'in the market-place' as lacking combination (2^{a}1), while, on the other hand, a single word which meant the same as 'white man' ought to count, in view of Chapter 4, as an expression involving combination. There seem to be two possible solutions. (*a*) The necessary and sufficient condition for an expression's being 'without combination' is that it should signify just one item in some category. The statement at the beginning of Chapter 4 is then analytic, but the examples in Chapter 2 are mis-leadingly selective, since on this criterion a single word could be an expression involving combination and a group of words could be an expression without combination. (*b*) The distinction in Chapter 2 is, as it looks, a purely linguistic one between single words and groups of words (or perhaps sentences). In Chapter 4 Aristotle neglects the possibility of single words with compound meaning and is indifferent to the linguistic complexity of expressions like 'in the Lyceum'. Certainly he does neglect single words with compound meaning in the rest of the *Categories*, though he has something to say about them in *De Interpretatione* 5, 8, and 11..

1ª20. The fourfold classification of 'things there are' relies on two phrases, 'being in something as subject' and 'being said of something as subject', which hardly occur as technical terms except in the *Categories*. But the ideas they express play a leading role in nearly all Aristotle's writings. The first phrase serves to distinguish qualities, quantities, and items in other dependent categories from substances, which exist independently and in their own right; the second phrase distinguishes species and genera from individuals. Thus Aristotle's four classes are: (*a*) species and genera in the category of substance; (*b*) individuals in categories other than substance; (*c*) species and genera in categories other than substance; (*d*) individuals in the category of substance.

Aristotle's explanation of 'in a subject' at 1ª24-25 is slight indeed. One point deserves emphasis. Aristotle does not define 'in *X*' as meaning 'incapable of existing separately from *X*', but as meaning 'in *X*, not as a part of *X*, and incapable of existing separately from what it is in'. Clearly the 'in' which occurs twice in this definition cannot be the technical 'in' of the definiendum. It must be a non-technical 'in' which one who is not yet familiar with the technical sense can be expected to understand. Presumably Aristotle has in mind the occurrence in ordinary Greek of locutions like 'heat in the water', 'courage in Socrates'. Not all non-substances are naturally described in ordinary language as *in* substances, but we can perhaps help Aristotle out by exploiting further ordinary locutions: *A* is 'in' *B* (in the technical sense) if and only if (*a*) one could naturally say in ordinary language either that *A* is in *B* or that *A* is of *B* or that *A* belongs to *B* or that *B* has *A* (or that . . .), and (*b*) *A* is not a part of *B*, and (*c*) *A* is inseparable from *B*.

The inseparability requirement has the consequence that only *individuals* in non-substance categories can be 'in' individual substances. Aristotle could not say that generosity is in Callias as subject, since there could be generosity without any Callias. Only this individual generosity—Callias's generosity—is *in* Callias. Equally, white is not in chalk as subject, since there could be white even if there were no chalk. White is in body, because every individual white is the white of some individual body. For a property to be in a kind of substance it is not enough that some or every substance of that kind should have that property, nor necessary that every substance of that kind should have it; what is requisite is that every instance of that property should belong to some individual substance of that kind. Thus the inherence of a property in a kind of substance is to be analysed in terms of the inherence of individual instances of the property in individual substances of that kind.

Aristotle does not offer an explanation of 'said of something as subject', but it is clear that he has in mind the distinction between individuals in any category and their species and genera. (Aristotle is willing to speak of species and genera in any category, though, like us, he most often uses the terms in speaking of substances.) He assumes that each thing there is has a unique place in a fixed family-tree. What is 'said of' an individual, X, is what could be mentioned in answer to the question 'What is X?', that is, the things in direct line above X in the family-tree, the species (e.g. man or generosity), the genus (animal or virtue), and so on. Aristotle does not explicitly argue for the view that there are natural kinds or that a certain classificatory scheme is the one and only right one.

It is often held that 'said of' and 'in' introduce notions of radically different types, the former being linguistic or grammatical, the latter metaphysical or ontological; and that, correspondingly, the word translated 'subject' (literally, 'what underlies') means 'grammatical subject' in the phrase 'said of a subject' and 'substrate' in 'in a subject'. In fact, however, it is perfectly clear that Aristotle's fourfold classification is a classification of things and not names, and that what is 'said of' something as subject is itself a thing (a species or genus) and not a name. Sometimes, indeed, Aristotle will speak of 'saying' or 'predicating' a *name* of a subject; but it is not linguistic items but the things they signify which are 'said of a subject' in the sense in which this expression is used in Chapter 2. Thus at 2^a19 ff. Aristotle sharply distinguishes things said of subjects from the names of those things: if A is said of B it follows that the name of A, 'A', can be predicated of B, though from the fact that 'A' is predicable of something it does not follow that A is said of that thing. At 2^a31-34 Aristotle is careless. He says that white is in a subject and is predicated of the subject; he should have said that white is in a subject and its name is predicated of the subject. But this is a mere slip; the preceding lines maintain a quite clear distinction between the things that are said of or in subjects and the names of those things. Being said of a subject is no more a linguistic property than is being in a subject—though Aristotle's adoption of the phrase 'said of' to express the relation of genus to species and of species to individual may have been due to the fact that if A is the genus or species of B it follows that 'A' can be predicated of B.

As regards 'subject', it is true that if virtue is said of generosity as subject it follows that the sentence 'generosity is (a) virtue'—in which the name 'generosity' is the grammatical subject—expresses a truth. But 'virtue is said of generosity as subject' is not about, and does not mention, the names 'virtue' and 'generosity'. It would be absurd to call generosity a *grammatical* subject: it is not generosity but 'generosity' that can be a grammatical subject. Again, if A is in B as subject then B is a substance. But this does not require or entitle us to take 'subject' in the phrase 'in a subject' as *meaning* 'substance' or 'substrate'. It is the expressions 'said of' and 'in' (in their admittedly technical senses) which bear the weight of the distinctions Aristotle is drawing; 'subject' means neither 'grammatical subject' nor 'substance', but is a mere label for whatever has anything 'said of' it or 'in' it. Thus at 2^b15 Aristotle explains his statement that primary substances are subjects for all the other things by adding that 'all the other things are predicated of them or are in them'.

The distinctions drawn in this chapter are made use of mainly in Chapter 5 (on substance). In particular, it is only in his discussion of substance that Aristotle exploits the distinction between individuals and species or genera. He seems to refer to individuals in non-substance categories at 4^a10 ff., but they are not mentioned in his chapters on these categories. Why does Aristotle not speak of primary and secondary qualities, &c., as he does of primary and secondary substances?

CHAPTER 3

1^b10. Aristotle affirms here the transitivity of the 'said of' relation. He does not distinguish between the relation of an individual to its species and that of a species to its genus. It does not occur to him that 'man' functions differently in 'Socrates is (a) man' and '(a) man is (an) animal' (there is no indefinite article in Greek).

1^b15. In the *Topics* (107^b19 ff.) Aristotle gives this principle about differentiae as a way of discovering ambiguity. If sharpness is a differentia both of musical notes and of solid bodies, 'sharp' must be ambiguous, since notes and bodies constitute different genera neither of which is subordinate to the other. At 144^b12 ff. he argues for the principle, saying that if the same differentia could occur in different genera the same species could be in different genera, since every differentia 'brings in' its proper genus. He goes on to water down the principle, allowing that the same differentia may be found in two genera neither of which is subordinate to the other, provided that both are in a common higher genus. In later works Aristotle preserves it as an ideal of classification and definition that the last differentia should entail all preceding differentiae and genera, although he recognizes that in practice we may fail to find such definitions and classifications (*Metaphysics* Z 12). In the *Metaphysics* Aristotle is motivated by a desire to solve the problem of the 'unity of definition' (*De Interpretatione* 17ª13), but no such interest is apparent in the *Topics* and *Categories*. Here he is probably influenced by the obvious cases of ambiguity like 'sharp', and also by the evident economy of a system of classification in which mention of a thing's last differentia makes superfluous any mention of its genus. Certainly the *Categories* gives no argument for the principle here enunciated. The principle may help to explain what Aristotle says about differentiae at 3ª21-28, ᵇ1-9.

The last sentence probably requires emendation. As it stands it is a howler, unless we take 'differentiae of the predicated genus' to refer to differentiae that divide it into sub-genera (*differentiae divisivae*) and 'differentiae of the subject genus' to refer to differentiae that serve to define it (*differentiae constitutivae*). But there is nothing in the context to justify such an interpretation. Only *differentiae divisivae* are in question. A correct point, following naturally from what goes before, is obtained if the words 'predicated' and 'subject' are transposed. That Aristotle is willing to describe the differentiae of a genus X as differentiae of the genus of X is clear; for he mentions two-footed as well as footed as a differentia of animal at 1ᵇ19, though the genus of which two-footed is an immediate differentia is not animal but a sub-genus of the genus animal.

CHAPTER 4

First, some remarks about the translation. 'Substance': the Greek word is the noun from the verb 'to be', and 'being' or 'entity' would be a literal equivalent. But in connexion with categories 'substance' is the conventional rendering and is used in the present translation everywhere (except in Chapter 1: 'definition of *being*'). 'Quantity': the Greek is a word that serves both as an interrogative and as an indefinite adjective (Latin *quantum*). If Aristotle made use also of an abstract noun it would be desirable to reserve 'quantity' for that; since he does not do so in the *Categories* (and only once anywhere else) it is convenient to allow 'quantity' to render the Greek interrogative-adjective. 'Qualification': Aristotle does use an abstract noun for 'quality' and carefully distinguishes in Chapter 8 (e.g. 10ᵃ27) between qualities and things qualified (Latin *qualia*). So in this translation 'quality' renders Aristotle's abstract noun, while his corresponding interrogative-adjective is rendered by 'qualified' or 'qualification'. 'A relative': Aristotle has no noun meaning 'relation'. 'A relative' translates a phrase consisting of a preposition followed by a word which can function as the interrogative 'what?' or the indefinite 'something'. In some contexts the preposition will be rendered by 'in relation to' or 'related to'. 'Where', 'when': the Greek words serve either as interrogatives or as indefinite adverbs ('somewhere', 'at some time'). 'Place' and 'time' are best kept to translate the appropriate Greek nouns, as at 4ᵇ24. 'Being-in-a-position', 'having', 'doing', 'being-affected': each translates an infinitive (which can be used in Greek as a verbal noun). The examples of the first two suggest that Aristotle construes them narrowly (posture and apparel), but the labels used are quite general. 'Being-affected' is preferred to alternative renderings because of the need to use 'affected' and 'affection' later (e.g. 9ᵃ28 ff.) as translations of the same verb and of the corresponding noun.

The labels Aristotle uses for his ten categories are, then, grammatically heterogeneous. The examples he proceeds to give are also heterogeneous. Man is a substance and cutting is a (kind of) doing; but grammatical is not a quality and has-shoes-on is not a kind of having. 'Grammatical' and 'has-shoes-on' are predicative expressions which serve to introduce but do not name items in the categories of quality and having.

How did Aristotle arrive at his list of categories? Though the items in categories are not expressions but 'things', the identification and classification of these things could, of course, be achieved only by attention to what we say. One way of classifying things is to distinguish different questions which may be asked about something and to notice that only a limited range of answers can be appropriately given to any particular question. An answer to 'where?' could not serve as an answer to 'when?'. Greek has, as we have not, single-word interrogatives meaning 'of what quality?' and 'of what quantity?' (the abstract nouns 'quality' and 'quantity' were, indeed, invented by philosophers as abstractions from the familiar old interrogatives); and these, too, would normally collect answers from different ranges. Now Aristotle does not have a category corresponding to every one-word Greek interrogative, nor do all of his categories correspond to such inter-rogatives. Nevertheless, it seems certain that one way in which he reached categorial classification was by observing that different types of answer are appropriate to different questions. This explains some of his labels for categories and the predicative form of some of his examples. The actual examples strongly suggest that he thinks about answers to questions about a *man*. Certainly he will have thought of the questions as being asked of a *substance*. This is why he often (though not in the *Categories*) uses the label 'what is it' as an alternative to the noun 'substance'. For what this question, when asked of a sub-stance, gets for answer is itself the name of a substance (cp. *Categories* 2^b31). One must not, of course, suppose that in so far as Aristotle is concerned to distinguish groups of possible answers to different ques-tions he is after all engaged in a study of expressions and not things. That 'generous' but not 'runs' will answer the question 'of-what-quality?' is of interest to him as showing that generosity is a different kind of thing from running.

Alternatively, one may address oneself not to the various answers appropriate to various questions about a substance, but to the various answers to one particular question which can be asked about any thing whatsoever—the question 'what is it?'. We may ask 'what is Callias?', 'what is generosity?', 'what is cutting?'; that is, we may ask in what species, genus, or higher genus an individual, species, or genus is. Repeating the same question with reference to the species, genus, or higher genus mentioned in answer to the first question, and continuing thus, we shall reach some extremely high genera. Aristotle thinks that substance, quality, &c., are supreme and irreducibly different genera under one of which falls each thing that there is. This approach may be said to classify subject-expressions (capable of filling the gap in 'what is . . .?') whereas the previous one classified predicate ex-pressions (capable of filling the gap in 'Callias is . . .'), though, as before, the point for Aristotle is the classification of the things signified by these expressions.

The only other place where Aristotle lists ten categories is in another early work, the *Topics* (I 9). Here he starts by using 'what is it' as a label for the category of substance. This implies the first approach, a classification derived from grouping the answers appropriate to different questions about some individual substance. But later in the chapter the other approach is clearly indicated. It is plain, Aristotle says, that 'someone who signifies what a thing is sometimes signifies substance, sometimes quantity, sometimes qualification, sometimes

one of the other predicates. For when a man is under discussion and
one says that what is being discussed is a man or is an animal, one
is saying what it is and signifying substance; whereas when the colour
white is under discussion and one says that what is being discussed
is white or is a colour, one is saying what it is and signifying qualification; similarly, if a foot length is being discussed and one says that
what is being discussed is a foot length, one will be saying what it is
and signifying quantity.' In *this* passage, where the question 'what
is it?' is thought of as addressed to items in *any* category, Aristotle can
no longer use 'what is it' as a label for the first category but employs
the noun for 'substance'. The whole chapter of the *Topics* deserves
study.

It is not surprising that these two ways of grouping things should
produce the same results: a thing aptly introduced in answer to the
question 'of-what-quality?' will naturally be found, when classified in
a generic tree, to fall under the genus of quality. The two approaches
involve equivalent assumptions. The assumption that a given
question determines a range of answers that does not overlap with
any range determined by a different question corresponds to the
assumption that no item when defined *per genus et differentiam* will be
found to fall under more than one highest genus. The assumption
that a certain list of questions contains all the radically different
questions that may be asked corresponds to the assumption that a
certain list of supreme genera contains all the supreme genera. It
should be noticed, however, that only the second method gets *individuals* into categories. For one may ask 'what is it?' of an individual in
any category; but items introduced by answers to different questions
about Callias are not themselves individuals, and a classification of
such items will have no place for Callias himself or for Callias's
generosity. It has, indeed, been suggested that individuals have no
right to a place in Aristotle's categories because the Greek word trans-
literated 'category' actually means 'predication' or 'predicate' (it is in
fact so rendered in this translation, e.g. 10^{b}21). However, it is substance, quality, quantity themselves which are the 'categories', that is,
the ultimate predicates; items belonging to some category need not be
items which can themselves be predicated, they are items of which
that category can be predicated. Thus the meaning of 'category'
provides no reason why Callias should not be given a place in a
category, nor why non-substance individuals should be left out.

Some general points: (1) Aristotle does not give argument to justify
his selection of key questions or to show that all and only the

genera in his list are irreducibly different supreme genera. When speaking of categories in other works he commonly mentions only three or four or five (which nearly always include substance, quantity, and quality), but often adds 'and the rest'. In one place he does seek to *show* that 'being' cannot be a genus, that is, in effect, that there must be irreducibly different kinds of being (*Metaphysics* 998ᵇ22). (2) Aristotle does not seem to doubt our ability to say what answers would be possible to given questions or to determine the correct unique definitions *per genus et differentiam* of any item we consider. When he looks for features peculiar to a given category (4ᵃ10, 6ᵃ26, 11ᵃ15) he does not do this to suggest criteria for categorial classification; his search presupposes that we already know what items fall into the category in question. He assumes also that we can tell which words or expressions signify *single* items rather than compounds of items from different categories. He does not explain the special role of words like 'species', 'predicate', &c., nor warn us against treating them, like 'animal' or 'generosity', as signifying items in categories. (3) Aristotle does not adopt or try to establish any systematic ordering of categories. Substance is, of course, prior to the rest; and he argues in the *Metaphysics* (1088ᵃ22) that what is relative is farthest removed from substance. (4) Aristotle does not in the *Categories* indicate the value of the theory of categories either for dealing with the puzzles of earlier thinkers or for investigating new problems. Nor does he, as elsewhere, develop the idea that 'is', 'being', &c. have different (though connected) senses corresponding to the different categories (*Metaphysics* 1017ᵃ22–30, 1028ᵃ10–20, 1030ᵃ17–27, *Prior Analytics* 49ᵃ7).

CHAPTER 5

2ᵃ11. The terms 'primary substance' and 'secondary substance' are not used in other works of Aristotle to mark the distinction between individual substances and their species and genera, though the distinction itself is, of course, maintained. The discussion of substance in *Metaphysics Z* and *H* goes a good deal deeper than does this chapter of the *Categories*. Aristotle there exploits the concepts of matter and form, potentiality and actuality, and wrestles with a whole range of problems left untouched in the *Categories*.

Aristotle characterises primary substance by the use of terms introduced in Chapter 2. But he does not, as might have been expected, go on to say that secondary substances are things said of a subject but not in any subject. Instead he describes them as the species and genera of primary substances and only later makes the point that they are said of primary substances but not in any subject. The reason for this may be that he is going to say (surprisingly) that the differentiae of substance genera, though not themselves substances, are nevertheless said of the individuals and species in the genera, and are not in them.

'Called a substance most strictly, primarily, and most of all': does Aristotle mean to suggest that 'substance' is used in two different *senses*? It would be difficult for him to allow that without upsetting his whole scheme of categorial classification. Aristotle is no doubt aware that the distinction between primary and secondary substances is not like that between two categories or that between two genera in a category; 'Callias is a primary substance' is unlike both 'Callias is a man' and 'Callias is a substance'. But he fails to say clearly what type of distinction it is.

2^a19. 'What has been said' presumably refers to 1^b10-15, which is taken to explain why, if A is said of B, not only the name of A but also its definition will be predicable of B. The first part of the paragraph is important as showing very clearly that the relation 'said of . . . as subject' holds between things and not words. The fact that A is said of B is not the fact that 'A' is predicable of B. The fact that A is said of B is not even the fact that both 'A' and the definition of A are predicable of B. This is a fact about language that follows from that fact about the relation between two things.

The second part of the paragraph is also of importance. It shows that Aristotle recognizes that, for example, 'generosity' and 'generous' do not serve to introduce two different things (we should say 'concepts'), but introduce the same thing in two different ways. In saying that usually the name of what is in a subject cannot be predicated of the subject he obviously means more than that, for example, one cannot say 'Callias is generosity'. He means that there is something else which one does say—'Callias is generous'—by way of ascribing generosity to Callias. His point would be senseless if 'generous' itself were just another name of the quality generosity or if it were the name of a different thing altogether.

2^a34. Someone might counter the claim in the first sentence by pointing out that, for example, animal is said of man and colour is in body, and man and body are *secondary* substances. Aristotle therefore examines just such cases. It is somewhat suprising that he says: 'were it predicated of none of the individual men it would not be predicated of man at all.' For in view of the meaning of 'said of' he could have made the stronger statement: 'were it not predicated of *all* of the

individual men. . . '. However, what he does say is sufficient for the
final conclusion he is driving at, that nothing else could exist if
primary substances did not. As for colour, Aristotle could have argued
to his final conclusion simply by using the definition of 'in' together
with the fact, just established, that the existence of secondary substances presupposes the existence of primary substances: if colour is
in body it cannot exist if body does not, and body cannot exist if no
individual bodies exist. What is Aristotle's own argument? It was suggested earlier that to say that colour is in body is to say that every
instance of colour is in an individual body. If so, Aristotle's present
formulation is compressed and careless. For he does not mention individual instances of colour; he speaks as if, because colour is in body,
colour is in an individual body. Strictly, however, it is not colour, but
this individual instance of colour, that is in this individual body; for
colour could exist apart from this body (though this instance of colour
could not). Aristotle's use of a relaxed sense of 'in' may be connected
with his almost complete neglect, after Chapter 2, of individuals in
non-substance categories.

In drawing his final conclusion in the last sentence Aristotle relies
partly on the definition of 'in' ('. . . cannot exist separately . . .');
partly on the principle that if A is said of B, A could not exist if B did
not. The closest he comes to arguing for this principle is at 3^b10–23,
where he insists that secondary substances are just *kinds of* primary
substance.

Aristotle's conclusion is evidently intended to mark out primary
substances as somehow basic (*contra* Plato). But the point is not very
well expressed. For it may well be doubted whether (Aristotle thinks
that) primary substances could exist if secondary substances and items
in other categories did not do so. But if the implication of existence
holds both ways, from the rest to primary substances and from primary
substances to the rest, the statement in the last sentence of his paragraph fails to give a special status to primary substances.

2^b7. The two arguments given for counting the species as 'more a
substance' than the genus—for carrying into the class of secondary
substances the notion of priority and posteriority already used in the
distinction between primary and secondary substances—come to
much the same. For the reason why it is more informative (2^b10) to
say 'Callias is a man' than to say 'Callias is an animal' (though both
are proper answers to the 'what is it' question, 2^b31–37) is just that the
former entails the latter but not vice versa: 'the genera are predicated

of the species but the species are not predicated reciprocally of the genera' (2^b20). The point of view is different at 15^a4–7, where it is said that genera are always prior to species since they do not reciprocate as to the implication of existence: 'if there is a fish there is an animal, but if there is an animal there is not necessarily a fish'. For this sense of 'prior' see 14^a29–35.

2^b29. Here the connexion between the 'what is it' question and the establishment of categorial lines is made very clear.

The second argument (from 'Further, it is because . . .') is compressed. Primary substances are subjects for everything else; everything else is either said of or in them (2^a34, 2^b15). Aristotle now claims that secondary substances are similarly related to 'all the rest', that is, to all things other than substances. This must be because all those things are *in* secondary substances. All Aristotle says, to establish this, is that 'this man is grammatical' entails 'a man is grammatical'. He means to imply that any non-substance that is in a primary substance is necessarily in a secondary substance (the species or genus of the primary substance). Since he has already argued that all non-substances are in primary substances he feels entitled to the conclusion that all non-substances are in secondary substances. But it will be seen that a further relaxation in the sense of 'in' has taken place. It is now implied, not only that generosity can be described as in Callias (though generosity could certainly exist in the absence of Callias), but also that generosity can be described as in man simply on the ground that some one man is generous (and not, as it strictly should be, on the ground that all instances of generosity are in individual men).

3^a7. Why is it 'obvious at once' that secondary substances are not *in* primary substances? It is not that they can exist separately from primary substances (2^a34–$^b6$). Nor does Aristotle appear to rely on the fact that a given secondary substance can exist separately from any given individual, that there could be men even if Callias did not exist, so that the species man can exist separately from Callias and is, therefore, not in him. Aristotle seems rather to be appealing to the obvious impropriety in ordinary speech of saying such a thing as 'man is in Callias'. It was suggested in the note on 1^a24–25 that Aristotle made it a necessary condition of A's being in B that it should be possible to say in ordinary non-technical discourse such a thing as 'A is in B' ('belongs to B', &c.). Now Aristotle is pointing out that this condition is not satisfied in the case of man and Callias. If this is his point he could have extended it to other categories; no genus or species in any category can naturally be described as in (or belonging to or had by) any subordinate genus, species or individual. What distinguishes secondary substances from non-substance genera and species is not that they are not in the individuals, species, and genera subordinate to them but that they are not in any *other* individuals, species, or genera; virtue is not in generosity, but it is in soul, whereas animal is not in man and not in anything else either.

One cannot say 'hero is in Callias' or 'father is in Callias'; but if Callias is a hero and a father the definition of 'hero' and 'father' can also be predicated of him. So it might be suggested that the considerations advanced by Aristotle in this paragraph imply that hero and father are secondary substances. But Aristotle is not claiming that any predicate-word which can be replaced by its definition is the name of a secondary substance (or differentia of substance, see below), but that a predicate-word can be replaced by the definition of the item it introduces if and only if the item is a secondary substance (or differentia of substance). 'Generous' can be replaced by the definition of 'generous'—but not by the definition of the item which 'generous' introduces, the quality generosity. Similarly, 'hero' and 'father' can be replaced by definitions of 'hero' and 'father', but not by definitions of the items they serve to introduce, heroism and fatherhood. Aristotle gives no explicit rules for deciding which common nouns stand for species and genera of substance (natural kinds) and which serve only to ascribe qualities, &c., to substances. He would presumably rely on the 'what is-it' question to segregate genuine names of secondary substances from other common nouns; but the question has to be taken in a limited or loaded sense if it is always to collect only the sorts of answer Aristotle would wish, and an understanding and acceptance of the idea of natural kinds is therefore presupposed by the use of the question to distinguish the names of such kinds from other common nouns which serve merely to ascribe qualities, &c. Surely it would often be appropriate to say 'a cobbler' in answer to the question 'What is Callias?'.

3^a21. The statement that something that is not substance is nevertheless said of substance is a surprising one, which can hardly be reconciled with the scheme of ideas so far developed. If the differentia of a genus is not a substance (secondary substances being just the species and genera of substance), it ought to belong to some other category and hence be in substance. That an item in one category should be said of an item in another violates the principle that if A

is said of B and B of C then A is said of C. Aristotle, indeed, positively claims that the definition as well as the name of a differentia is predicable of the substance falling under it, but this too seems very strange. In a definition *per genus et differentiam* the differentia is commonly expressed by an adjective (or other non-substantive), and this should surely be taken to introduce an item named by the corresponding substantive (as 'generous' introduces but is not the name of generosity). If we say that man is a rational animal 'rational' brings in rationality, but neither the name nor the definition of rationality can be predicated of man. Thus the differentiating property satisfies a test for being *in* substance (cp. $2^a19\text{--}34$).

Aristotle is no doubt influenced by the following facts. (1) Species and genera of individual substances are themselves called substances because 'if one is to say of the individual man *what* he is, it will be in place to give the species or the genus' (2^b32). If we now consider the question 'what is (a) man?' we shall be strongly inclined to mention not only the genus animal but also the appropriate differentia. The differentia seems to be *part of* the 'what is it' of a secondary substance, and this provides a strong motive for assimilating it to substance even while distinguishing it from species and genera. (2) The principle enunciated at 1^b16 implies that mention of a differentia renders superfluous (to one who knows the true classification of things) any mention of the genus. To ascribe the differentia 'two-footed' to man is as good as to say that he is a two-footed land animal. Thus the differentia is, in a way, the *whole* of the 'what is it' of a secondary substance. (3) Aristotle uses as examples of differentia-words words which function naturally in Greek as nouns (though they are strictly neuter adjectives). At $14^b33\text{--}15^a7$ he uses the same words when speaking explicitly of *species* (and so they are translated there by 'bird', 'beast' and 'fish'). Moreover, there are in Aristotle's vocabulary no abstract nouns corresponding to these neuter adjectives (as 'footedness', 'two-footedness'). Such facts are far from establishing that the definition as well as the name of a differentia is predicated of substances. For not all differentiae are expressed by nouns or words used as nouns, and abstract nouns corresponding to differentia-words are not always lacking. In any case, there are plenty of nouns (like 'hero') which Aristotle would insist on treating as mere derivatives from the names of the things they introduce ('heroism'); and the fact that there is no name for, say, a quality does not exclude the possibility that some predicative expression serves to ascribe that quality (though not, of course, paronymously: 10^a32--^b5). Thus, that 'footed' is (used as) a noun and no noun 'footedness' exists is not a justification for refusing to treat 'footed' in the same kind of way as 'hero' or 'generous', as introducing a characteristic neither the name nor the definition of which is predicable of that which is footed. Nevertheless, the above features of the examples he hit upon may have made it somewhat easier for him to say what he does about differentiae without feeling the need for full explanation. For deeper discussion of the relation of differentia to genus, and of the connected problem of the unity of definition (referred to at *De Interpretatione* 17ᵃ13), see especially *Metaphysics* Z 12.

3ᵃ33. 'All things called from them are so called synonymously': Aristotle is not denying that there are words which stand ambiguously for either of two kinds of substance (like 'animal' in Chapter 1). Things to which such a word applied in one sense would not be 'called from' *the same substance* as things to which it applied in the other sense; and Aristotle is claiming only that all things called from any given substance are so called synonymously, not that all things called by a given substance-word are necessarily so called synonymously.

Aristotle is drawing attention again to the following point (it will be convenient to assume that there is no sheer ambiguity in the words used). There are two ways in which something can be called from the quality virtue: generosity is a virtue, Callias is virtuous; neither the name nor the definition of virtue is predicable of Callias. There are two ways in which something can be called from the quality white: Della Robbia white is (a) white, this paper is white; the name but not the definition of white is predicable of this paper. There is only one way in which something can be called from man: Callias is a man, Socrates is a man, and so on; both the name and the definition of man are predicable of Callias and Socrates and so on.

It is not quite clear that Della Robbia white and this paper are homonymous with respect to the word 'white', in the meaning given to 'homonymous' in Chapter 1. For there the case was that the word (e.g. 'animal') stood in its two uses for two different things with two different definitions. Now, however, we have 'white' in one use standing for a thing (a quality) which has a certain definition, but in the other use not standing for a different thing with a different definition but introducing differently the very same thing. However, an easy revision of the account in Chapter 1 would enable one to say that 'synonymously' in the present passage contrasts with both 'homonymously' and 'paronymously': most non-substances (like generosity) generate paronymy, a few (like the quality white) generate homonymy; no substance generates either.

'From a primary substance there is no predicate': there is no subject of which Callias is said or in which Callias is. In the *Analytics* Aristotle speaks of sentences in which the name 'Callias' is in the predicate place, and says that this is only accidental predication (43^a34, cp. 83^a1-23). He does not make any thorough investigation of the different types of sentence in which a proper name may occur in the predicate place. Nor does he discuss such uses as 'he is a Socrates', 'his method of argument is Socratic'. He would no doubt allow that these are cases of genuine predication but deny that the predicates are 'from a primary substance': the connexion between the characteristics ascribed by '. . . is a Socrates' and '. . . is Socratic' and the individual Socrates is purely historical and contingent; we should not have used '. . . is a Socrates' as we do if there had been no Socrates or if Socrates had had a different character, but we could perfectly well have used a different locution to ascribe the very same characteristics. A similar answer would be available if someone claimed that there are after all two ways in which something may be called from a secondary substance since while Tabitha is *a cat* Mrs. So-and-so is *catty*. It is because of real or assumed characteristics of cats that the word 'cattiness' names the characteristics it does; but the characteristics themselves could have existed and been talked about even if there had never been any cats.

3^b10. Aristotle has contrasted individual substances with their species and genera. He has labelled the latter 'secondary' and has argued that their existence presupposes that of primary substances. Nevertheless, much that he has said provides a strong temptation to think of species and genera of substance as somehow existing in their own right like Platonic Forms. In the present passage Aristotle tries to remedy this. It is careless of him to speak as if it were substances (and not names of substances) that signify. More important, it is unfortunate that he draws the contrast between a primary substance and a secondary substance by saying that the latter signifies a certain qualification. For although he immediately insists that 'it does not signify simply a certain qualification, as white does', yet the impression is conveyed that secondary substances really belong in the category of quality. This, of course, Aristotle does not mean. 'Quality of substance' means something like 'kind' or 'character of substance'; it derives from a use of the question 'of what quality?' different from the use

which serves to classify items as belonging to the category of quality.
'Of what quality is Callias?' (or 'what kind of person is Callias?') gets
answers from the category of quality. But 'what quality of animal is
Callias?' (or 'what kind of animal is Callias?') asks not for a quality
as opposed to substance, quantity, &c., but for the quality-of-animal,
the kind-of-animal. It is a result of the limitations of Aristotle's
vocabulary that he uses the same word as a category-label and to
convey the idea of a kind, sort or character of so-and-so. (Cp. *Metaphysics* 1020ª33–ᵇ1, 1024ᵇ5–6, where 'quality' refers to the differentia
—in any category—not to the *category* of quality.) It is also clear that
he is at a disadvantage in this passage through not having at his dis-
posal such terms as 'refer', 'describe', 'denote', 'connote'; and that he
would have been in a better position if he had from the start examined
and distinguished various uses of expressions like '(a) man' instead of
embarking at once upon a classification of 'things there are'.

3ᵇ24. Aristotle raises the question of contrariety in each of the
categories he discusses. On the suggestion that large and small are
contraries see 5ᵇ11–6ª11.

3ᵇ33. The question of a more and a less is raised in each category.
'We have said that it is': 2ᵇ7. There is a certain ambiguity in 'more',
since to say that a species is more a substance than a genus is to assign
it some sort of priority but not to ascribe to it a higher degree of some
feature as one does in saying that this is more hot than that.

The point Aristotle makes here about substances applies also, of
course, to sorts which he would not recognize as natural kinds: one
cobbler or magistrate is not more a cobbler or magistrate than another.

4ª10. What Aristotle gives here as distinctive of substance is strictly
a characteristic of *primary* substances. For he is not speaking of the
possibility of man's being both dark and pale (of there being both dark
men and pale men), but of the possibility of one and the same individual man's being at one time dark and at another time pale. (It
will then be distinctive of secondary substances that the individuals of
which they are said are capable of admitting opposites.) Correspondingly, Aristotle must be meaning to deny, not that species and genera
in other categories may in a sense admit contraries (colour may be
white or black), but that individual instances of qualities, &c., can
admit contraries while retaining their identity. His first example is
not convincing. An individual instance of colour will necessarily be
an instance of some specific colour and will be individuated accord-

ingly: if X changes from black to white we first have X's blackness and then X's whiteness, *two* individuals in the category of quality. (To this there corresponds the fact that one and the same individual substance cannot move from one species to another.) What is required is to show —not that X's blackness cannot retain its identity while becoming white, but—that X's blackness cannot retain its identity while having contrary properties at different times. The sort of suggestion Aristotle ought to rebut is, for example, the suggestion that one and the same individual instance of colour could be at one time glossy and at another matt, this variation not making it count as different instances of *colour*. Aristotle's second example is of the right kind, since the goodness or badness of an action does not enter into the identity-criteria for an individual action in the way in which the shade of colour does enter into the identity-criteria for an individual instance of colour. However, the example is still particularly favourable for him. For 'good' and 'bad' are commonly used to appraise an action *as a whole*, and for this reason one would not speak of an action as having been good at first and then become bad. There are clearly very many cases which it would be less easy for Aristotle to handle (cannot an individual sound sustain change in volume and tone?). The question demands a fuller scrutiny of cases and a more thorough investigation of usage than Aristotle attempts. It would seem that the power to admit contraries is not peculiar to individual substances but is shared by certain other continuants, so that a further criterion is required to explain why these others are not counted as substances.

4ᵃ22. Aristotle of course treats the truth and falsity of statements and beliefs as their correspondence and lack of correspondence to fact (4ᵇ8, 14ᵇ14–22, *Metaphysics* 1051ᵇ6–9). Here he first points out that it is not through a change in itself that a statement or belief at one time true is at another time false, whereas an individual substance itself changes; so that it remains distinctive of primary substances that they can admit contraries *by changing*. He next argues (4ᵇ5) that strictly a thing should be said to admit contraries only if it does itself undergo a change from one to the other; so that, strictly speaking, it is not necessary to qualify what was said at 4ᵃ10–11: only individual substances can admit contraries.

Aristotle might have argued that the alleged counter-examples, individual statements or beliefs which change their truth-value, fail, because my statement now that Callias is sitting and my statement later that Callias is sitting are not the same *individual* statement even

if they are the *same statement* (just as 'a' and 'a' are two individual instances of the same letter). Thus they are not examples of the very
same individual admitting contraries. Alternatively, Aristotle could
have denied that the statement made by 'Callias is sitting' when
uttered at one time *is* the *same statement* as that made by 'Callias is
sitting' when uttered at another time. The sameness of a statement
or belief is not guaranteed by the sameness of the words in which it
is expressed; the time and place of utterance and other contextual
features must be taken into account.

CHAPTER 6

In Chapter 8 Aristotle distinguishes between *qualities* and things
qualified or *qualifications* of things (between 'generosity' and 'the generous' or '. . . is generous'); his primary concern is with qualities, of
which he distinguishes four main types. His treatment of quantity,
in Chapter 6, is different in two ways. First, he uses no abstract noun
for 'quantity' but employs everywhere the interrogative-adjective; see
beginning of note on Chapter 4. Secondly, he does not list or attempt
to classify quantitative properties (like the property of being a foot
long) or corresponding quantitative predicates (like 'a foot long').
Instead he lists and groups the *owners* of quantitative properties, claiming to list all the (primary) owners of such properties: lines, surfaces,
solids, numbers (aggregates), time-periods, places, utterances. Why
does he proceed like this, and can his procedure serve as an adequate
way of classifying quantitative properties?

As for the first question, some linguistic facts may be relevant. There
were not numerous abstract nouns corresponding to the various
quantitative predicates, as there were in the case of qualitative predicates. Such general terms as 'length', 'area', and 'time' were ambiguous: a line, for example, could be said to be *of* a certain length,
but it could also itself be called a length. Definite predicates like 'a foot
long' could not easily be regarded as introducing quantitative properties fitting in to a genus–species hierarchy. (How many species would
there be in the genus length, and what would be their differentiae?)
Aristotle does not stop to examine carefully the nature of counting and
measuring, nor does he survey the different ways in which quantity or
quantities may be spoken of; and he does not recognize explicitly the
inappropriateness of the genus–differentia-species model to the
category of quantity. Such facts as the above may, however, have
influenced him towards adopting the approach he does to the problem
of classifying quantities.

As for the adequacy of Aristotle's method, it is clear that under certain conditions a list of owners of quantitative properties might provide an exhaustive and mutually exclusive classification of types of quantitative property: if the list includes one (non-derivative) owner for each type of quantitative property, and if each kind of owner listed admits only one type of quantitative property. It is easier to fulfil the second condition than the first. A (geometrical) *line* has no quantity but length, an *aggregate* as such has only a number. Compare the Euclidean definition 'a line is length without breadth', and Aristotle's *Metaphysics* 1020ª13: 'limited plurality is a number, limited length is a line, area a surface, volume a solid'. The second condition can be fulfilled when there are terms which, in ordinary or technical use, are logically tied to just one type of quantitative property, as 'line' is in geometry. The first condition can be met only if such a term is available for each and every type of quantitative property. It seems that this is not so and that, consequently, Aristotle fails to give a list of primary owners of quantitative properties which secures an exhaustive classification of such properties. Thus he had no word related to weight as 'line' to length. That such terms could be invented only brings out, what is already obvious, that the fundamental reason for distinguishing different types of quantitative property is not that there are different kinds of 'thing' each found to admit a different range of quantitative predicates; we have names for such 'things' just because it is convenient to study ownership of one type of quantitative property in abstraction from others. The use of words like 'line' in geometry presupposes discovery of and interest in length as one particular type of quantitative property. The real explanation of our discriminating different types of quantitative property must be sought in the purposes and techniques of counting and measuring and in the progressive discoveries of science.

Aristotle does not discuss the status of lines, &c., in his own categorial scheme. They are obviously not substances, though they have properties. Their relation to primary substances is not at all elucidated in the *Categories*.

With this chapter should be compared the chapter on quantity in *Metaphysics* Δ (c. 13). On the unit and the relation between counting and measuring see specially *Metaphysics* I 1 and N 1.

4ᵇ20. The notion of continuity is discussed at length in the *Physics* (V 3, VI 1-2). The only elucidation in the present work is in the phrase 'the parts join together at a common boundary'.

Why does Aristotle deny continuity to numbers? (a) There is clearly no sense in saying that the number 3 touches or (what is stronger) joins on to the number 4. But Aristotle ought not to be making this point here, for when he lists numbers with lines, surfaces, &c., it is surely numerable aggregates that he must have in mind, not the number 3 and the number 4. (b) An aggregate need not consist of items that touch one another; whether they do or not is irrelevant when they are counted. But Aristotle is saying not that something need not be the case with aggregates but that something cannot be the case. Also, he is talking not of touching but of joining together. Perhaps then he has in mind that two things that join together at a common boundary thereby constitute one thing, so that if they are to constitute a pair of things they must not join together. If so, he overlooks the possibility of looking at the same objects in different ways: the fingers of a hand join together to make one hand, but they remain five fingers. (c) A set of ten things consists of two sets of five; but it does not make sense to ask where the common boundary is. Equally, however, if one says that a 10-inch line consists of two 5-inch lines it does not make sense to ask where the junction is, since no particular actual line is being spoken of. One can, indeed, be sure that the two halves of any actual 10-inch line will join at a point; but then one cannot be sure that *no* set of ten things will consist of two sets of five which do join together at a common boundary. So this again would not provide the contrast Aristotle seeks to establish.

Aristotle's inclusion of spoken language as a primary quantity seems odd. The length or shortness of a syllable—what we still call its *quantity*—is a matter of the length or shortness of time taken by its utterance; so speech is not a primary, non-derivative owner of quantitative properties.

In saying that the present time (literally, 'the now time') joins on to past and future time Aristotle treats it as itself having duration. In the *Physics* IV 11 he argues that the now is a limit or boundary; it is no *part* of time, any more than the points are parts of the line; time is made continuous by the now, and divided at it.

Place is defined in the *Physics* IV 4 as the limit of the containing body. The proof given here that place is continuous treats it similarly as filled by (or perhaps only fillable by) a body. This raises the question whether place has a right to count as an independent primary quantity in addition to body.

5^{a}15. It will be seen that the line of division between discrete and continuous quantities corresponds to that between quantities whose parts lack and quantities whose parts have relative position, except in the case of time, which is continuous but whose parts lack relative position. This may be why *Metaphysics* Δ 13, which treats time as only a derivative quantity, makes no use of the position-test for classifying quantities.

For the parts of a quantity to have position relative to one another requires, apparently, that each part should have spatial location ('lies somewhere') and that each part should join on to another part. The latter requirement obviously prevents any non-continuous quantity from consisting of parts having position relative to one another, while the former is clearly sufficient to prevent time from consisting of such parts. It is therefore surprising that Aristotle invokes the fact that the parts of time and of utterances are *transient* as a ground for saying that they cannot have relative position. The appeal 'how could what is not enduring have any position?' hardly has the obvious knock-out force that Aristotle supposes, and it is certainly superfluous since the appropriate classification of time and utterance could be more simply achieved as indicated above.

What does Aristotle mean by saying that the parts of a number have order in that one is counted before two and two before three? He ought not to mean simply that the numbers 1, 2, 3, &c., form an ordered series; for it is aggregates of which he should be speaking, and an aggregate—say, the Hungarian trio—does not have the numbers 1, 2, 3 as parts. Perhaps he means that in counting the players in the group we necessarily take them one by one; we order them as we count, saying 'one', 'two', 'three'. The members of the group do not have an order as the numbers in the number-series do, but they are given an order, taken in order, when they are counted, that is, when they are treated as parts of a numerable aggregate. If this is what Aristotle has in mind he might have done better to say that the first is counted before the second and the second before the third rather than that one is counted before two and two before three. Perhaps, however, he means that in counting a group we necessarily count increasingly large sub-groups: Tom (as we say 'one'), Tom and Dick (as we say 'two'), Tom, Dick, and Harry (as we say 'three'), and so on. These sub-groups fall into an order, each containing the preceding sub-group together with one extra individual; a sub-group of two members must be counted before a sub-group of three members can be. We can take the individuals in the group in any order we like, but we must have counted some trio before we can count a quartet. On this account there are of course far more than n 'parts' in an aggregate of n individuals since each sub-group is also a part; indeed all the 'parts of a number' which 'have a certain order', except for the first part (the individual we take first in counting), will themselves be sub-groups of the whole group being counted.

5^a38. Aristotle is surprisingly dogmatic here. Contrast the last lines of Chapter 7 and 10^a25–26. An adequate analysis and classification of quantitative properties is impossible without a preliminary study of the nature of counting and measurement, and this Aristotle does not attempt. His distinction between 'strict' and 'derivative' quantities may be thought to contain the germ of the crucial distinction between fundamental and derivative processes of measurement (which will be found discussed in any good modern treatment of measurement), but Aristotle does not develop the idea at all fully.

5^b11. Aristotle has so far been talking about owners of quantitative properties. He now considers a question about quantitative properties themselves (or quantitative predicates). He is not saying that a line has no contrary, but that two-foot has no contrary; not that two mountains cannot be contraries, but that large and small are not contraries. His use of the word 'surface' at 5^b13 is misleading; he must mean 'area'.

In 5^b15–29 Aristotle argues that large and small are not quantities but relatives (so that even if they were contraries they would not count against the statement that no quantity has a contrary). In 5^b30–6^a11 he argues that large and small are not in fact contraries (so that even if they were quantities they would not count against the statement that no quantity has a contrary).

There appear to be two arguments to show that large and small are relatives, but it is hard to find a second independent argument in lines 26–29 ('Further, . . .'). Aristotle's main point is valuable, though it is over-simple to construe 'large mountain' as 'mountain larger than other mountains'. 'Large, judged by the standard of size appropriate for mountains' does not mean the same as 'larger than all—or most—other mountains', even though there is obviously a close connexion between the standard taken as appropriate and the actual sizes of known mountains.

Aristotle's treatment of 'large' as having the force of 'larger than . . .' and therefore being a relative term raises some questions. (a) Could not the same treatment be given to some terms which

Aristotle is happy to regard as not relative? Thus the criteria for bravery in a soldier and for bravery in a girl are different, and a soldier braver than most girls would not necessarily qualify as a brave soldier; so should not 'brave' count as a relative term if 'large' does? (b) Granted that 'larger than' and 'braver than' are relative terms, would it not be natural to distinguish the former as quantitative from the latter as qualitative? Would it not be possible to parcel out all relatives among other categories rather than to segregate them as one category beside all the rest? (c) If 'larger than' is a relative term, what about 'larger than most mountains'? Aristotle would presumably say that this is neither a quantity nor a relative, but that it expresses a compound and not a single item of the sort that finds a place in a category. But if so, the same might be said of 'two-foot'. For to say that something is two-foot is to say that it is twice as long as a foot; and though 'twice as long as a foot' is more definite than 'larger than a foot' or 'larger than most mountains', it consists, as they do, of a relative term and a *relatum*. Because Aristotle has not attended in the *Categories* to the role of the unit in measurement he fails to notice the possibility of breaking down definite quantitative predicates in the manner suggested.

5^b30. At first sight it would seem that at $5^b30–33$ Aristotle assumes that large and small *are* relatives while claiming to show that they are not contraries 'whether one counts them as quantities or does not', that is, even if they are taken to be quantities and *not* relatives. In fact, however, all he assumes is the feature ('by reference to something else') which he used above (5^b17) as proof that large and small were relatives. Here he claims that whether or not that feature proves them to be relatives it anyway proves them not to be or to have contraries. Why should he think this obvious? He will himself allow that relatives can be contraries (6^b15), so he cannot suppose that every type of relatedness excludes contrariety. But he does not explain the exact kind of 'reference to something else' which large and small involve, nor show why that kind of relatedness does exclude contrariety.

Aristotle next argues that the assumption that large and small are contraries leads to two absurd consequences: that a thing can admit contraries simultaneously, and that something can be its own contrary. As to the former, Aristotle is neglecting the restrictions which (as he often remarks) must be incorporated if the principle about contraries is to be acceptable. A thing cannot admit contraries at the same time *and* in the same respect *and* in relation to the same thing,

&c. (See Plato's formulation and discussion in *Republic* 436.) When so formulated the principle does not serve Aristotle's purpose. That a thing can be at the same time large in comparison with one thing and small in comparison with another does not prove that large and small are not contraries. Aristotle himself indeed holds that knowledge and ignorance are contraries ($6^{b}15$), yet the same person can at the same time both know (one thing) and be ignorant (of another); the restrictions on the principle about contraries which prevent this from being an absurdity also annihilate the first of Aristotle's alleged absurdities about large and small.

The second *reductio ad absurdum* ($6^{a}5$: 'It turns out also . . .') is evidently not fully stated. For the stated premisses, that large and small are contraries and that the same thing is both large and small at the same time, do not yield the conclusion that something is its own contrary (which must mean not that a thing can have two contrary properties—which was the first absurdity—but that two contrary properties can be identical). Nor would the desired conclusion be reached by adding, as a third premiss, the principle that nothing can admit contraries at the same time. Perhaps the following line of thought is implied:

(1) large and small are contraries ($6^{a}5$);
(2) a thing is both large and small at the same time ($6^{a}6$);
(3) contraries are in the same genus ($6^{a}17$);
(4) large and small are in the same genus (from (1) and (3));
(5) nothing can admit different properties from the same range at the same time (a more general version of the principle of non-admissibility of contraries);
(6) large and small are identical (from (2), (4), and (5));
(7) contraries can be identical with one another (from (1) and (6)).

Since (7) is absurd but (2), (3), and (5) are correct, (1) must be false.

$6^{a}11$. Aristotle thinks of 'up' and 'down' as naming two places (the outside and centre of the world) and secondarily applying to things according as they move towards or are relatively near to one or the other of the fixed extremes. Since in any case 'up' and 'down' would not give the quantity of anything (but rather its 'where' or 'whither') the view that they are contraries does not seem to justify the suggestion that there is after all contrariety in quantity.

With $6^{a}17$–18 contrast $14^{a}19$–25.

$6^{a}19$. This point, like that about contrariety, concerns quantitative properties or predicates. Aristotle is not saying that one line is not

more *a line* than another, but that one line is not more *two-foot* than
another. He is careless when he says 'Nor yet is one time called more
a time than another'; he should say that one time or period of time is
not, for example, more *a year long* than another. His reference to 'those
we listed' is also unhappy, since those were lines, surfaces, &c., but
we are now concerned with quantitative predicates or properties, not
with their owners.

6ª26. Here Aristotle does have in mind owners of quantitative properties. Compare *Metaphysics* 1021ª11: 'Those things are the *same* whose
substance is one; those are *similar* whose quality is one; those are *equal*
whose quantity is one.' Two lines are equal if they are of one and the
same length. It is surprising that Aristotle fails to notice that 'equal'
and 'unequal' can be applied in a derivative way to things that are
not strictly but only derivatively called quantities (compare 5ᵇ6–8 on
'white' with 6ª33). In any case an examination of the uses of 'equal'
and 'unequal' (in Greek or English) soon shows the inadequacy of
this as a distinguishing mark of those things Aristotle counts as
quantities.

CHAPTER 7

As has been said (p. 78), Aristotle has no noun for 'relation' but
exploits a preposition having the force 'relative to', 'in relation to'.
In this chapter he does not, for the most part, treat of relations (similarity, slavery) but rather, in effect, of relational predicates ('similar',
'slave'). He does not himself put the matter in this linguistic way.
He does not say that 'larger' and 'slave' are relatives, but that the
larger and the slave are relatives. However, he does not, of course,
mean that, for example, the slave Callias is a relative (he is a substance), but that Callias is a relative in so far as he is *called a slave*;
in other words, 'slave' is a relative term. The distinction between
relations or relational properties and relatives is drawn at the end of
the chapter on relatives in *Metaphysics* Δ (1021ᵇ6–8); 'further, there
are the properties in virtue of which the things that have them are
called relative, for example, equality is relative because the equal is,
and similarity because the similar is.'

6ª36. 'Of' and 'than' represent the Greek genitive. Aristotle first
gives examples of terms followed by the genitive, and then (6ᵇ8–10)
gives examples of terms followed by some other case or by a preposi-
tional phrase.

What is larger is called larger than something. 'Callias is larger' is clearly incomplete. It need not be unintelligible, since the context of utterance may make clear with whom or what Callias is being compared; it is then elliptical. The case is different with 'Callias is a slave'. This is perfectly intelligible without knowledge of context, though it has a certain indefiniteness; it is equivalent to 'Callias is the slave *of someone*'. Aristotle does not bring out this difference between 'Callias is larger' and 'Callias is a slave' (though he has something to say about definiteness later, 8ª35 ff.). Another distinction we might look for *could* not be drawn in Greek, that between 'larger' and 'larger than'; for the 'than' represents not a word but the genitive case-ending of the word following 'larger'.

It is not clear why Aristotle proceeds to say that state, condition, perception, knowledge, and position are relatives. Knowledge and perception are of the knowable and perceptible (6ᵇ34–36, 7ᵇ23 ff.). But with 'state', 'condition', and 'position' it is not obvious what Aristotle means by saying that they are followed by genitives. A state is necessarily the state of someone or something. But if this were all Aristotle had in mind he would be committed to treating all non-substance terms as relatives, since every non-substance must be 'in' a substance: generosity must be someone's generosity. Perhaps Aristotle means that a state must be the state of bravery or the state of generosity, &c.; perhaps the genitive he has in view is specificatory. However, it is certainly not obligatory in Greek for 'state', &c., to be followed by such a genitive (indeed it is uncommon); while if Aristotle is really concerned, not to insist on the genitive-requirement, but to insist that a state must be a state of some specific kind, then again he will be committed to counting as relatives a vast number of terms (generic terms) which he in fact puts into other categories. One might think of other possible criteria for counting 'state', &c., as relatives, but what Aristotle has in mind remains uncertain. There is an important reference to states and conditions as relatives at the end of Chapter 8, but the passage does not solve the present problem. It does explain the meaning of 'and not something different' (6ᵇ4): grammar is not a relative because though it is called *knowledge of* something it is not called *grammar* of something.

On 'large mountain' see 5ᵇ15–29 and note.

6ᵇ11. It is not clear whether the first sentence intends to convey that lying, standing, and sitting are relatives or that they are not. If the latter, the point will be the same as that of 11ª20 ff. With the second sentence compare [11ᵇ10–11] and 12ª35–39.

6^b15. The words here and elsewhere rendered 'virtue' and 'vice' can be taken more widely—'goodness' and 'badness'. It is not clear whether Aristotle classifies them here as relatives because a virtue must be the virtue of bravery or of generosity, &c., or whether he means more generally that goodness must be goodness at something, for something, in some sphere or capacity, &c.

On contrariety in relatives see 5^b30 ff. and note.

6^b28. In this and the following paragraphs Aristotle maintains that if the correlative of a relative (literally 'that in relation to which the relative is spoken of') is correctly given, it will always be found to reciprocate. The requirements for being correctly given are implied at $6^b39–7^a3$, $7^a7–10$ and $16–18$ (and, in a rather different form, at $7^a24–^b9$, with which compare *Topics* $149^b4–23$). The claim that A and B reciprocate is the claim that 'X is A of (to, than, &c.) Y' entails 'Y is B of X' and 'Y is B of X' entails 'X is A of Y'. Thus 'parent' and 'child' reciprocate, but 'parent' and 'son' do not, nor do 'father' and 'child'. Aristotle is in fact discussing *converse* relations (or the relative terms that express such relations). He insists that the proper correlative of any relative term is that which expresses the converse relation, and he holds that there always is such a converse though there may be no name for it (he might have added that there may be more than one name for it).

$6^b36–7^a22$ is concerned with *parts* of animals and things. He will later argue that 'wing', 'rudder', &c., are not after all relatives $(8^a28–^b21)$.

7^b15. On 'simultaneous by nature' see $14^b27–33$. In *Metaphysics* Δ 15 Aristotle mentions the knowable, the perceptible and the measurable as examples of a special kind of relative, and he tries to explain their peculiarity $(1020^b30–32, 1021^a26–^b3)$. More helpful is his discussion in *De Anima*, where he exploits the distinction between potentiality and actuality: the actualizations of perception and of the perceptible are necessarily simultaneous (and indeed one and the same, though conceptually distinct), but the two potentialities are not. 'The actuality of the perceptible and that of perception are one and the same (though their being is not the same). I mean, for example, actual sound and actual hearing: it is possible for one who has hearing not to be hearing, and what has a sound is not always sounding; but when what can hear is actually doing so and what can sound is sounding, then the actual hearing and the actual sound (which one might call hearkening and sounding respectively) occur simultaneously. . . . Since the actuality of the perceptible and of that which can perceive is one (though their being is different), it is necessary for hearing and sound, understood in this way, to cease to exist or continue to exist simultaneously—and so also savour and taste, and so on; but understood as potentialities they do not necessarily do so. Earlier students of nature did not give a satisfactory account of this, for they thought that without sight there was nothing either white or black, and without taste no savour. What they said was right in one way, not right in another. For perception and the perceptible are spoken of in two ways, sometimes as potentialities, sometimes as actualities; and while their statement holds for the latter, it does not hold in the former cases' (425^b25-426^a1, 426^a15-25).

8^a13. When Aristotle says that an ox is not called someone's ox, he obviously means that an ox is not necessarily someone's ox (as a piece of property is necessarily someone's property), not that it is linguistically improper to say that an animal 'is someone's ox'. With primary substances, however, his point is probably different. He probably means to suggest that it is linguistically improper to attach possessive genitives to designations of primary substances: one cannot say that something is 'Callias's this ox', though one can, of course, say that this ox is Callias's (ox).

8^a28. Aristotle now seeks to evade the necessity of classifying certain substances (namely, parts such as heads and hands) as relatives by introducing a revised criterion for being a relative. The new criterion is found elsewhere, e.g. at *Topics* 142^a29, 146^b3. Ever since antiquity there has·been controversy about the interpretation of this criterion and about the difference between it and the earlier one. The following facts are undeniable:

(a) according to Aristotle the first criterion makes heads and hands relatives while the second does not;
(b) the first criterion refers to what is *said*, what things are *called*, while the second does not (hence the traditional terms *secundum dici* and *secundum esse*);
(c) Aristotle says that whatever satisfies the second criterion also satisfies the first (8^a33);
(d) the second criterion is said to have a consequence concerning the necessity of 'knowing definitely' that to which something is

related (8^a35–37), and the fact that this necessity does not hold in the case of heads and hands is taken to show that they are not, by the revised criterion, relatives (8^b15-19).

It is (d) that seems to hold out most promise of clarifying the distinction between the two criteria. Aristotle appears to be saying this: on the first (weaker) criterion for being a relative R one could know that A was R without knowing what it was R of, though it would necessarily be R of something; whereas on the second (stronger) criterion one could know that A was R only if one knew what it was R of. However, this would make the strong criterion too strong, since it would not be satisfied by indisputably relative terms like 'half' and 'slave': one can know that 97 is half some other number without knowing what that number is, and that Callias is a slave without knowing who his master is. We might try watering down the strong criterion so as to allow that one may know that A is R without knowing what it is R of, it being required only that *someone* knows what it is R of or that one (or someone) *could* find out what it is R of. But now the criterion is satisfied by 'hand' and 'head' as well as by 'half' and 'slave', given that a hand or head must be someone's hand or head. Alternatively we might stress the phrase 'definitely know' and legislate that one cannot 'definitely know' that 97 is half another number and that Callias is a slave unless one knows what the number is and who the master is. But then no reason is apparent why this requirement should be waived in other cases, that is, why it *should* be possible to 'definitely know' that this is a hand without knowing whose hand it is. It will hardly be claimed that the ordinary usage of 'definitely know' guarantees the distinction—that everyone familiar with the phrase will immediately see that 'definitely knowing that Callias is a slave' entails 'knowing who Callias's master is' while 'definitely knowing that this is a hand' does not entail 'knowing whose hand this is'.

Could Aristotle have this point in mind, that while a slave must actually be someone's slave a rudder need not actually be part of a boat though it must be capable of serving as part of a boat? 'Boat' will occur in the definition of 'rudder', but a thing may be and be known to be a rudder without its being (yet, still, or ever) a component of an actual boat. It is hard to read this into Aristotle. The examples he gives after stating the first criterion at the beginning of the chapter seem to be straightforward cases of incompleteness ('larger . . .', 'similar . . .'); there is no hint that the criterion would be satisfied by terms which have only the sort of definitional dependence which 'rudder' has on 'boat'. Again, 8^a35-^b19 does not suggest the contrast that a slave must be somebody's slave whereas a head may be nobody's head; it concerns the necessity or otherwise of one's *knowing* whose slave a slave is and whose head a head is. Moreover, Aristotle's choice of examples ('head' and 'hand') tell against the suggestion under discussion. For bodiless heads and hands are a good deal less usual than rudders not incorporated into boats, and if Aristotle's point had to do with actual separability he would probably bring in an obviously favourable example like 'rudder' instead of or as well as the less obviously favourable 'head' and 'hand'. Indeed, according to a well-known Aristotelian doctrine, a severed (or dead) hand is not, strictly speaking, a hand at all; a hand is a functioning organ of a living body. 'The parts of a body cannot exist if severed from the whole; for it is not a finger in any and every state that is the finger of a living thing, but a dead finger is a finger only in name' (*Metaphysics* 1035^b23-25). 'When seeing is removed the eye is no longer an eye, except in name—it is no more a real eye than the eye of a statue or of a painted figure' (*De Anima* 412^b20-22). 'The whole is necessarily prior to the part. For if the whole is destroyed there will not be a foot or a hand except homonymously (as if one were to speak of a stone hand, for a hand when destroyed will be like that); all things are defined by their function and capacity, so that when they are no longer such they should not be said to be the same things, but homonymous' (*Politics* 1253^a20-25). We cannot be sure that Aristotle held this view when he wrote the *Categories* (though compare the statement of *De Interpretatione* 21^a23 that 'dead man' implies a contradiction); certainly if he did he could not have allowed the suggestion that heads and hands are actually separable from bodies.

CHAPTER 8

8^b25. 'Quality' translates the abstract noun coined (probably by Plato, *Theaetetus* 182 a) from a familiar old word which served as both an interrogative and as an indefinite adjective (Latin *quale*). Where Aristotle uses this latter word it is translated by 'qualified' or 'qualification'. He uses it mainly to refer to qualities-as-ascribed-to-things, or, to put it more plainly, when he is thinking of 'generous' and 'sweet' as opposed to 'generosity' and 'sweetness'. When he says that in virtue of a quality we are 'said to be qualified' (9^a32, $^b23$, 27, &c.) he does not mean that we are described as 'qualified' but that we are described by a qualification-word, by a word ('generous', 'pale') which is a proper answer to the question 'how qualified?'. If an adjective is a proper answer to the question '*quale?*' the corresponding noun names a *qualitas*.

When Aristotle says that quality is 'spoken of in a number of ways' he does not mean that the word 'quality' is ambiguous but only that there are different kinds of quality. He proceeds to list and discuss four kinds. He does not 'deduce' them or connect them on any principle, nor does he insist that there are no other types of quality (10^a25-26).

8^b26. The word here translated 'state' is so translated everywhere except in Chapter 10, where it is used in the different sense of 'possession' as opposed to 'privation'. The word here translated 'condition' is so translated everywhere.

It will be seen that Aristotle uses 'condition' in a narrow and a wide sense, first contrasting states with conditions and then treating states as a sub-class of conditions (8^b27-9^a10, 9^a10-13). He gives no special argument to show that states and conditions are qualities. Nor does he give any criterion for deciding that a given quality is or is not a state-or-condition; why, for example, should affective qualities be treated as a class quite distinct from that of states and conditions?

To distinguish between states and conditions Aristotle relies on at least two criteria, length of time and changeability. He seems to require that a state should both last a long time and be hard to change, and that a condition should not last long and should be easily changed. He does not tell us what to say in cases where the two criteria pull apart. A man's good health might chance to persist for a long time without, however, becoming 'part of his nature and irremediable or exceedingly hard to change'; a man might acquire a firm grasp of some branch of knowledge ('hard to change') and yet lose it—if 'a great change is brought about by illness or some other such thing'—before he has had it for a long time. Are these men to be described as in states or in conditions? It may be that Aristotle introduces yet a third criterion: 'quickly changing' suggests a contrast between relatively sudden and relatively gradual alterations, and this is not the same as the contrast between alterations easy and difficult to bring about. Perhaps, however, 'quickly changing' means only 'not lasting long'.

Aristotle does not clearly distinguish two ways in which his (or similar) criteria might be used. (1) They might be used to draw up two lists of qualities: *A, B, C, . . .* are states, *M, N, O, . . .* are conditions. Suppose justice is one of the states. Then unless a man consistently keeps the laws over a long period he cannot be called just: since justice is a state, not a condition, it cannot be ascribed to some- one unless his conduct is consistent over a long period. (2) The criteria might be used to distinguish cases where we are to say that a man is in the state X from cases where we are to say that a man is in the condition X. If X is justice then a man can be said to be in the *state* of justice only if his conduct is consistent over a long period, but he can be said to be in the *condition* of justice in virtue of his conduct over a short period.

9^a14 There is no great difficulty in understanding 'a natural capacity or incapacity to do or suffer something easily', but it is surprising that Aristotle treats this as a distinct type of quality while saying nothing about capacities in general. One may have or lack an aptitude for trigonometry; but to say that someone is capable of learning trigo- nometry is not to ascribe or deny an aptitude to him. Something may be fragile or the reverse; but to say that something is breakable is not to say that it is or is not easy to break. So 'capable of learning trigo- nometry' and 'breakable' do not stand for type 2 qualities, but Aristotle does not say where they do belong in his classification. Again, what about *acquired* capacities or abilities? Would Aristotle count them as qualities of the first kind—states or conditions? Evidently there are many different distinctions that ought to be drawn: between abilities, on the one hand, and inclinations, traits of charac- ter, states of mind and body, &c., on the other; between mere possibility and positive proneness, liability, aptitude, &c.; between natural and acquired abilities; between abilities to do or suffer some- thing and abilities to acquire or retain abilities to do or suffer some- thing; and so on. Aristotle's mapping of this territory is not very thorough.

The boxer who is so called because of a natural ability to do something easily is distinguished by Aristotle from the boxer who is so called in virtue of his 'condition', that is, because he has learned the science of boxing (10^b1-3). But it is not clear whether the natural ability in question is the ability to fight well without training or the ability to acquire skill through training. If the latter, there is an important similarity between the boxer or runner (where natural capacity is meant) and the healthy or sickly person. For the healthy person is one able to keep in health, and the sickly person is one pre- disposed not to keep in health. Thus both 'boxer' (or 'runner') and 'healthy' (or 'sickly') will refer to abilities to acquire or keep type 1 qualities, in one case knowledge or skill, in the other case health. It is, however, doubtful whether 'hard' and 'soft' can be so treated: it is not clear that to have been divided is to be in a certain state or condition.

9ª28. Aristotle's first examples make one expect that 'affective qualities' will mean 'sensible qualities' ('productive of an affection of the senses', 9ᵇ6). But his strange suggestion as to why complexion colourings are called *affective* qualities leads him to extend the class of affective qualities far beyond sensible ones. The distinction which he draws in the course of his excursus on complexions between affective qualities and affections gets applied to psychological characteristics. Affective qualities now include qualities of mind or temperament which are due to congenital or otherwise unalterable or compelling 'affections'. It is clear that Aristotle's bizarre theory about complexions has led him to introduce into his philosophical classification of qualities an unnecessary and unusable empirical criterion. The distinction between the irascible man and the man who on some trying occasion loses his temper is of course a good one. But if irascibility is to be classified as an *affective* quality it should surely be because the irascible man is one who is *prone* to suffer a certain affection (to lose his temper) or because the *criterion* for calling a man irascible is that he has often suffered this affection. The congenital *causes* of irascibility should be left to the physiologist or psychologist. (In any case, of course, 'affective' is being used in two ways: the irascible man is certainly not a man who *produces* affections.)

Aristotle starts by calling affections qualities (9ª28) but ends by saying they are not qualities (10ª10). He says that people are not, in virtue of affections, said to be qualified somehow (9ᵇ29). Now it is clear that 'he is blushing' and 'he is in a rage' are not proper answers to the question '*qualis?*' ('how is he qualified?', 'what is he like?'); they say rather how he is being affected. But Aristotle does not seem to be distinguishing 'is blushing' and 'is in a rage' from 'is red-faced' and 'is bad-tempered'. He seems to be distinguishing the case where 'is red-faced' or 'is bad-tempered' describes a man's permanent or normal state from the case where they describe a temporary condition due to a temporary cause. He seems to be saying that if Callias is temporarily red-faced or bad-tempered it would not be right to answer the question 'what is Callias like?' by saying that he is red-faced or that he is bad-tempered. This is a fair point, but it hardly justifies the conclusion that temporary high colour or bad temper are not qualities at all. We can ask what Callias is like *now*, and it seems unreasonable to deny that the answers 'red-faced' and 'bad-tempered' indicate qualities simply because they may apply to Callias only temporarily and as a result of some temporary cause. After all, Aristotle allows that short-lived *conditions* are qualities; yet one would not mention them in answer to the temporally unrestricted question 'what is Callias like?' It seems, in short, to be one thing to distinguish the category of quality from other categories (including that of being-affected), and another thing to examine the conditions for mentioning qualities of various kinds in reply to questions of various forms (e.g. temporally restricted and temporally unrestricted).

How can Aristotle include hotness and coldness in this group of qualities (9^a30) when he has already classified them as conditions (8^b36–39)? An acute discussion in *De Partibus Animalium* (648^b11–649^b8) distinguishes several senses of 'hot' but does not provide an answer to the present question. Perhaps the conditions Aristotle has in mind are the conditions of *feeling* hot or cold; one may feel hot without being hot to another's touch, that is, without possessing the corresponding affective quality.

With 9^b14 ff. compare *Prior Analytics* 70^b7-38.

10^a11. 'Shape' perhaps refers to properties of geometrical lines and surfaces, 'the external form of each thing' to the configurations of physical objects.

10^a16. Aristotle denies that 'open-textured', &c., signify qualifications, holding that they indicate rather the position of a thing's parts. Might not the same be said of words for the various shapes or external configurations of things? Moreover, it is not obvious that a word meaning 'composed of parts arranged in a certain way' cannot be a proper answer to the question 'how qualified?'; it is not clear into which category Aristotle would wish to put openness of texture, roughness, &c.

10^a27. On 'paronymously' see Chapter 1 and note.

10^b17. 'Predicates' here evidently refers to the list of categories (see p. 80). The point made seems to have no special relevance to the category of quality: whatever category one of a pair of contraries is in, its contrary will no doubt be in the same category.

10^b26. Aristotle attributes to 'some people' a thesis about conditions, this word being used in its wide sense. Their point seems to be the very general one that one cannot say that one X-ness is more an X-ness than another. If so, it has nothing to do with conditions in particular but concerns abstract nouns (or what they name). One might wonder whether they wish to distinguish some qualities from others according to whether it is or is not possible to speak of degrees of the quality. It might be suggested that there are not degrees of justice or health (but only degrees of approximation to these perfect states) whereas there are degrees of injustice and ill-health. The text, however, does not justify attributing this view to the people mentioned.

11^{a}15. Aristotle is not saying that if two things share a quality they can properly be described as similar (without qualification); only things which share many qualities or the most important ones can be so described (*Metaphysics* 1018^{a}15 ff.). He is saying that if two things can properly be described as somehow similar then the feature in respect of which they are similar is a quality. There is in fact a close etymological connexion between the word translated 'similar' and the word meaning 'qualified'.

11^{a}20. This is a perplexing passage. The claim that a genus that is a relative may have species that are not relatives seems to conflict with Aristotle's whole idea of a genus-species classification and categorial ladders. So too does the suggestion (11^{a}37) that the same 'thing' may be in two categories. The underlying difficulty is perhaps this, that grammar (that is, knowledge-of-grammar) is not a proper species of knowledge. Contrast the division of knowledge into species which Aristotle gives at *Topics* 145^{a}13–18: 'the differentiae of relatives are themselves relatives, as with knowledge; for it is called theoretical and practical and productive, and each of these signifies a relative.' This division of knowledge, into the species theoretical knowledge, practical knowledge and productive knowledge, is, of course, radically different from a division by subject-matter; it raises no categorial problem, since the species are themselves relatives for the same reason that the genus is. Compare a division of 'multiple' into 'double', 'treble', &c. (*Topics* 121^{a}4). Aristotle would surely not wish to count 'multiple of 3' as a species of 'multiple'; should he not also deny that knowledge of grammar is a species of knowledge, and so side-step the question how the species can fail to be a relative when its genus is by denying that any cases of this have been produced? There would, however, remain for him a serious problem. What *is* he to say about expressions like 'knowledge of grammar' and 'multiple of 3'? Does such an expression introduce a single item to be located in some category, or is it to be treated as a compound which introduces two items belonging to two different categories? There are strong reasons to take the former view. 'Knowledge of grammar' and 'multiple of 3' are clearly not mere conjunctions of names of different items, like 'white man'; 'Callias knows grammar' cannot be decomposed as 'Callias is a white man' can (into 'Callias is white' and 'Callias is a man'). Moreover, such expressions can answer the questions which serve to discriminate categories ('knowledgeable about grammar' can answer the question '*qualis?*'), so each such expression should stand for an item in the appropriate category; and a vast number of the items Aristotle does classify into categories are or might be designated by expressions of this kind (e.g. the capacity to resist sickness). On the other hand, the assumption that each such expression stands for a single item with a place in one category leads to a difficulty. For it seems impossible to find a place in the species–genus–category hierarchy for the things which 'knowledge of grammar' and 'multiple of three' are supposed to stand for. Thus there is a nasty dilemma, and its existence points to a weakness in the foundations of Aristotle's theory of categories.

CHAPTER 9

See the Introductory Note.

CHAPTER 10

11^{b}17. Aristotle regularly uses this fourfold classification of opposites. See, for example, *Topics* II 8 and V 6, *Metaphysics* 1054^{a}23, 1055^{a}38, 1057^{a}33.

11^{b}24. Cp. 6^{b}28–7^{b}14. Aristotle uses here the terminology of his first criterion for being a relative, but it cannot be inferred that he wrote this paragraph before he had worked out the revised criterion which he gives towards the end of Chapter 7. For all terms that satisfy the revised criterion also satisfy the first one (8^{a}33); thus he can say what he does say in this paragraph even if he has in mind the revised criterion for being a relative.

11^{b}38. 'The things they naturally occur in or are predicated of': after 12^{b}29 Aristotle uses the blanket term 'belong to'. 'Occur in' and 'are predicated of' do not seem to draw the same distinction as that between 'in' and 'said of' in Chapter 2.

'Such that it is necessary for one or the other of them to belong': cp. *Posterior Analytics* I 4 (73^{a}37-^{b}5, ^{b}16–24) on *per se* attributes.

12^{a}26. On privation and possession see, for example, *Metaphysics* $\varDelta$ 22 and 1046^{a}31–35.

12^{a}35. Cp. 6^{b}11–14 and Plato's *Theaetetus* 156 e. The argument 'Moreover, if . . . ' is not carefully stated; there is a switch from 'being blind' to 'blind'.

'What underlies an affirmation': at *De Interpretatione* 21^{b}26–32 Aristotle speaks of man and white as the 'subject things' (literally, 'underlying things') of the statement 'man is white'; here, however, it is the whole thing that is asserted (e.g. his sitting, man's being white) that is described as underlying the statement.

12^{b}26. Aristotle has distinguished above (11^{b}38–12^{a}25) between two types of contraries. If A and B are type 1 contraries and X a thing capable of receiving them, X must at all times have either A or B. If C and D are type 2 contraries and X a thing capable of receiving them, X need not at any time have either C or D. Aristotle now introduces an alternative possibility for type 2 contaries: if C and D are type 2 contraries and X a thing capable of receiving them, *either* (a) X need not at any time have either C or D, *or* (b) X must at all times have definitely C or must at all times have definitely D. By contrast, if E and F are possession and privation and X a thing capable of receiving them, X need not at all times have either E or F (contrast type 1 contraries) but it must at some time have either E or F (contrast type 2 contraries, case (a))—though 'not definitely one or the other of these' (contrast type 2 contraries, case (b)). It will be seen that this last addition is really superfluous. Possession and privation are already sufficiently distinguished from cases of type 2 (b) by the fact that a thing capable of receiving a possession or privation may at some time lack both, for this is not true of cases of type 2 (b). The whole analysis can, of course, be made much more perspicuous if expressed in modern logical symbolism.

13^{a}37. 'Necessary always for one to be true . . .': but see *De Interpretatione* 17^{b}29–30, 18^{a}10, 18^{a}31–33.

In the last sentence Aristotle slides from talking of health, sickness, &c., to talking of 'health', 'sickness', &c. On 'said without combination' see 1^{a}16, 2^{a}4–10, *De Interpretatione* 16^{a}9–18, 17^{a}17–20.

13^{b}12. The accusative and infinitive phrase which Aristotle here uses to refer to a statement ('Socrates is well') is later (14^{a}10) used to refer to a state of affairs (Socrates's being well). The translation makes clear a distinction that was perhaps not so clear to Aristotle.

Does Aristotle maintain that the non-existence of the subject always makes an affirmative statement false and a negative one true, or does he have in mind only singular statements? How, in any case, is this view to be reconciled with the contention at *De Interpretatione* 21ª25–28 that 'Homer is a poet' does not entail 'Homer is'?

'One or the other of them will be true or false': Aristotle clearly means that one will be true and one will be false.

CHAPTER 11

13ᵇ36. 'But what is contrary to a bad thing is sometimes good but sometimes bad': or rather, some bad things have both a good contrary and a bad contrary. The type of case Aristotle has in mind is discussed in *Nicomachean Ethics* II 8.

14ª19. Compare 6ª17, *Topics* 123ᵇ1 · 124ª9, *Metaphysics* 1018ª25–35, 1055ª3–33. 'Contraries in contrary genera' means 'contraries whose *immediate* genera are contrary'. If these contrary genera are themselves in one and the same higher genus then the original contraries are also both in the same genus, but not immediately. 'Good and bad are not in a genus': does Aristotle mean that they are not in any *ordinary* genus (but fall immediately under a category), or that they are not in any one category because 'good' like 'being' occurs in all the categories (*Nicomachean Ethics* 1096ª23–29, *Topics* 107ª3–17)? If the latter is Aristotle's point he does not express it very well by saying that good and bad 'are themselves genera'.

CHAPTER 12

On priority and posteriority see *Metaphysics* Δ 11.

14ª26. 'Reciprocate as to implication of existence': cp. Chapter 13 on 'simultaneous by nature', and 7ᵇ15–8ª12.

'The elements are prior in order to the diagrams': the definitions, postulates and axioms of geometry are prior to the propositions. Many geometrical 'propositions' are in fact solutions to construction-problems (e.g. Euclid I 1, 2, 3); and the construction of appropriate *diagrams* plays an important role even in the proofs of theorems (e.g. the theorem of Pythagoras, Euclid I 47).

14ᵇ9. On the relation between facts and truth compare *De Interpretatione* 18ª39–ᵇ3, 19ª33–35, and *Metaphysics* 1051ᵇ6–8: 'It is not because we think truly that you are pale, that you are pale; it is because you are pale that we who say this are speaking truly.' It is odd to call this a reciprocal implication of *existence*: we should not say that the existence of there being a man implies and is implied by the existence of the true statement that there is a man, nor does Aristotle adhere to this way of speaking in his discussion of the example.

'Cause': or 'reason'. Aristotle has one word for both.

CHAPTER 14

15ª13. Aristotle holds that there is change in just four categories: in substance (generation and destruction), in quantity (increase and diminution), in quality (alteration), and in place (motion). See *Physics* 200ᵇ33. At *Physics* 260ª26—ᵇ7 he argues that change of place is presupposed by alteration and that alteration is presupposed by increase; but that thesis does not conflict with the claim in the present passage that the six kinds of change are all distinct from one another and that what is undergoing one is not necessarily undergoing any other.

'For generation is not destruction, nor yet . . .': Aristotle here shows, by listing and rejecting possible identifications, that *destruction* is not the same as any of the other kinds of change (that is, any of the other *four*—alteration is to be considered separately). He claims that a similar procedure will establish for each of the other kinds that it too is not identical with any other ('similarly with the others too').

15ᵇ1. Compare *Physics* V 5, 6.

CHAPTER 15

This chapter is not a discussion of the *category* of having but a survey of various uses of the very common verb 'have': cp. *Metaphysics* Δ 23.

DE INTERPRETATIONE

CHAPTER I

16ᵃ1. This is the programme for Chapters 2-6. Comment on the terminology and on the English renderings chosen will be found in the notes on those chapters.

16ᵃ3. This account of the relation of things in the world, affections in the soul, and spoken and written language is all too brief and far from satisfactory. What precisely are 'affections in the soul'? Later they are called thoughts. Do they include sense-impressions? Are they, or do they involve, images? Aristotle probably calls them likenesses of things because he is thinking of images and it is natural to think of the (visual) image of a cat as a picture or likeness of a cat. But the inadequacy of this as an account or explanation of thought is notorious. Again, what is it for a spoken sound to be a 'symbol' of something in the mind? And are written marks symbols of spoken sounds in the same sense in which these are symbols of thoughts? Is it necessary —or only natural—to regard speech as primary and writing as secondary?

There are grave weaknesses in Aristotle's theory of meaning. Fortunately, the notion that utterances are symbols of affections in the soul and that these are likenesses of things does not have a decisive influence on the rest of the *De Interpretatione*. For example, Aristotle does not often appeal to psychological experiences or facts to explain or support what he says about names, verbs, statements, &c.; most of what he says is independent of the special theory about words, thoughts, and things.

Aristotle's main and official discussion of thinking (to which he— or an editor—here refers us) is in *De Anima* III 3–8.

The present passage is intended as an argument for the view that language is conventional (cp. 16ᵃ19, 16ᵃ26, 16ᵇ33): different people (or peoples) confront the same things and situations, and have the same impressions of them and thoughts about them (likeness is a natural relation); but they use different spoken or written words to express their thoughts (words are conventional symbols). Of course it is not true that all men meet the same things or have the same thoughts.

Nor would the mere fact that different words are equally capable of expressing a given thought be enough to prove that words are significant only by convention, not by nature. (The choice of material for an axe is *not* a matter of convention; the nature of an axe's task imposes limits. Yet there may be a variety of materials any of which would do—though not every material would do. Thus the possibility of different people's using differently made tools for the same job does not show that it is purely a matter of convention how a tool for that job is made.) Aristotle would have made his point more cogently if he had said that different men *may* share the same thought though expressing it in different words, and that there is *no* restriction on what sounds or written marks could be used by people as words to express their thoughts. The whole question whether language is conventional or natural is brilliantly discussed in Plato's *Cratylus*.

16ᵃ9. Single names or verbs, like the thoughts they stand for, are neither true nor false (cp. *Categories* 2ᵃ4, *De Interpretatione* 16ᵇ19, 17ᵃ9, ᵃ17); to have a truth-value a thought, and hence a linguistic expression, must involve a combination or separation (cp. *Metaphysics* E 4. 1027ᵇ17–28). Of course, not every kind of combination in an expression ensures it a truth-value: prayers are not true or false (17ᵃ3) nor are mere phrases (17ᵃ11). It is the statement or statement-making sentence that is true or false (17ᵃ2), because it either affirms or denies something of something (c. 6).

Aristotle supports the statement that a noun or verb by itself cannot be true or false by taking an example of a name that might seem a strong candidate for a truth value. Since the name 'goat-stag' applies to nothing it might be thought to be (always) false. But this is not so. One who says 'goat-stags' has after all not said 'goat-stags exist'; this or some other verb must be added before there is anything true or false. (The main point about 'goat-stag' is that it applies to nothing, but the fact that it is a compound word is not irrelevant to the preceding discussion: not every type of combination guarantees truth-value to an expression.)

The suggestion that thoughts are likenesses of things is not acceptable even for simple thoughts like the thought of a cat. It is even less acceptable for thoughts that would be expressed in sentences. My thought that the cat will soon wake is hardly a 'likeness' of a thing or complex of things, even if it is true; and the situation is still more desperate if it is false. The problem how there could possibly be false belief or statement had exercised many Greek philosophers, and in the

Sophist Plato had gone a long way towards solving it. In speaking of thoughts as likenesses of things Aristotle uses just the kind of model which had caused chronic perplexity. The very example he uses illustrates the difficulty; of what is the thought of a goat-stag a likeness?

What is meant by 'either simply or with reference to time'? One might suppose that 'simply' alludes to the timeless or to the omnitemporal present tense. But there is nothing to support this elsewhere in the work. Chapter 3 draws a sharp distinction between present time and past and future times, and Aristotle may have that distinction in mind here—though it would not be very happily expressed by the disjunction 'either simply or with reference to time'.

CHAPTER 2

16ᵃ19. 'Name' gives the original and central meaning of the Greek *onoma* and it has been used everywhere in the present translation. In some contexts it is tempting to write 'word' or 'noun', but only 'name' can do duty in all contexts. Moreover, the use of 'name' in the translation will serve to remind the reader of the rather primitive nature of Aristotle's view of meaning: 'Philo' and 'man' are names of different sorts of thing but are both just names.

'A spoken sound significant by convention' gives the genus under which fall not only names but also verbs (Chapter 3) and phrases and sentences (Chapter 4). As was to be expected from 16ᵃ3, Aristotle deals with spoken, not written, language. The linguistic items he wishes to consider are marked off from sounds not spoken, from spoken sounds that are not significant, and from spoken sounds that are natural signs (e.g. certain animal calls and cries—the word rendered 'spoken sound' has a wider range of application than the English expression). 'None of whose parts is significant in separation' applies to verbs as well as names, and marks them off from phrases and sentences. 'Without time' distinguishes names from verbs.

16ᵃ21. This passage and 16ᵇ28–33 have to do with the distinction between single words (names or verbs) and phrases or sentences. What are the criteria for counting an expression as a *word, one* word? Aristotle's remarks are brief and at the most important point obscure; for he does not explain what he means by saying of a part of an expression that it does, or that it does not, have significance in that expression 'in its own right' or 'in separation'. In discussing this it will be convenient to consider written rather than spoken expressions. A 'part' of an expression *E* will then be any letter of *E* (unless *E* is itself a single letter) or any block of consecutive letters taken from E (but not the whole of E). The following seem safe: (a) if a significant expression E is such that no part of E, when written on its own, is significant, then E is a word; e.g. 'cut', 'rag'. (b) If a significant expression E is such that no part of it, when written on its own, has a significance that contributes to the significance of E, then E is a word; e.g. 'mice', carpet'. Aristotle does not explicitly distinguish these two types of case, but he seems to give an example of each in Chapter 4. Of the word represented in the translation by 'animal' ('animal' has the relevant linguistic properties of the Greek word though it does not mean the same) Aristotle says that the single syllables signify nothing —case (a). But with regard to the example (represented by) 'mice' he says that *here* 'ice' is simply a spoken sound; that is, by itself 'ice' is significant, but it does not carry that significance when it forms a part of 'mice'—case (b).

We now come to cases where Aristotle's terms 'in its own right' and 'separately' come into play. These are cases where some part of E, when written on its own, has a significance—and a significance that does contribute to the meaning of E—although when that part is written not on its own but as a part of E it does not carry significance 'in its own right' or 'separately'. How are we to decide whether such a part of an expression (let us call it a contributorily meaningful part) is a word in a phrase or sentence, or only a bit of a single compound word? Aristotle's example translated 'pirate-boat' suggests one sufficient condition for saying that such a part is not, when written as a part of E, a word. For the removal of either of the contributorily meaningful parts 'pirate' and 'boat' leaves a sequence of letters that cannot stand on its own as a significant unit (assuming that we count '-' as a letter): 'pirate-', '-boat'. (Aristotle's example does not in fact involve a hyphen; it is more like 'thermometer'.) A satisfactory formulation of this point would be a matter of some complexity, but the general idea is clear enough. One can establish that in 'lemonade', 'pirateer', and 'thermometer', 'lemon', 'pirate', and 'meter' are not functioning as separate words (even though they can so function and even though they do contribute to the meaning of the compounds 'lemonade', &c.) by pointing out that 'ade', 'er', and 'thermo' *cannot* stand alone as significant expressions. In Aristotle's terminology, 'pirate' in 'pirateer' is not significant 'in its own right' or 'in separation', that is, it is not serving as an independent word. A reason for saying this is that 'er' certainly is not, since it never can be, serving as an independent word.

Many compound words, however, though far fewer in Greek than in English, cannot be treated along the lines suggested for 'pirateer' (or 'pirate-boat', provided '-' is treated as a letter). Plenty of compound words can be exhaustively divided into parts each of which is contributorily meaningful and each of which can function alone. How are we to decide in such cases whether the parts, when written as parts of *E*, do or do not 'signify in their own right'—whether *E* is one compound word or rather a phrase? Why do we count (and write) 'bookcase' as one word, 'brown case' as two? Aristotle does not use any example like 'bookcase', and it would be inappropriate to pursue the topic further here.

It is a pity that Aristotle introduces a proper name (represented by 'Whitfield') as an example of a compound. Proper names clearly require special treatment. Whitfield may have acquired his name because he or his father owned a white field; but this is a merely historical fact and has nothing to do with the present use or 'significance' of 'Whitfield'.

Mention should be made of the grammatical excursus in *Poetics*, cc. 20–21, which discusses compound words, names, verbs, &c. The chapters are, however, full of difficulty, and they will not be further referred to in these notes.

16^a26. The second sentence is meant to support the first. But though it shows that it is not a sufficient condition for a sound's being a name that it should 'reveal' something, it does not show that a necessary condition is that it should be conventional. Aristotle only weakens the force of his remark by mentioning *inarticulate* noises, that is, such as do not consist of clearly distinguishable sounds which could be represented in writing. For someone could suggest that what prevents such noises from counting as names is not that they are natural rather than conventional signs, but precisely that they are inarticulate. Aristotle should have said rather that sounds made by animals, even when they reveal something and *are* clearly articulated, are nevertheless not counted as names. Even this, of course, would not prove that their failure is due to their not being conventional.

16^a29. 'Not man' is certainly not a negation, that is, a negative statement (cp. 20^a31–36); it is less clear why Aristotle denies that it is a phrase. If his reason for not counting it as a name *simpliciter* were that it is not a single word this should make it count as a phrase. Probably he thinks of it as a single word but thinks that it fails to name anything in the way in which an ordinary name does: it stands for no definite kind of thing and can be applied to a wildly various range of objects. Cp. 19ᵇ9: 'for what it signifies is in a way one thing, but indefinite.' (In the translation it will normally be convenient to write 'not-man', though there is no hyphen in the Greek.)

16ᵃ32. Aristotle here excludes oblique cases of nouns from counting as names by adding a further condition: a name joined to 'is', 'was', or 'will be' always constitutes a true or false sentence. The 'is' here, as in the last sentence of Chapter 1, is to be taken in an existential sense. Greek has one verb for the copulative 'is' and for 'exists'; and since this generated philosophical problems it is usually best for a translator to preserve the ambiguity by using 'to be', 'is', &c., even where the natural English would be 'to exist', 'exists'.

Why does Aristotle so restrict the notion of a name? He is not interested in a purely grammatical classification of parts of speech (which would naturally count all cases of nouns as nouns) but in the analysis of simple statements. Following Plato (*Sophist* 262) he thinks of such a statement as consisting of a subject-expression which is the name of something and a predicate-expression which says something about the thing named. Oblique cases of names cannot perform as subject-expressions, cannot play the naming role in a sentence.

CHAPTER 3

16ᵇ6. The original meaning of the word translated 'verb' is simply 'what is said'. In Plato's and Aristotle's analysis of the simple statement the word stands for the part that says something about that which the subject-expression, the name, names. In the simplest cases this part is one word, a verb, and since it is such cases that Aristotle starts with and has in mind in this chapter the translation 'verb' seems best. It may disturb us to find Aristotle saying that a statement consists of a name and a verb, because this terminology suggests a confusion of logical with grammatical analysis. But this is not a confusion imported by the translation; logic and grammar are, in fact, not clearly distinguished in Aristotle's discussion.

A verb is distinguished from a name in two ways. A name is 'without time', a verb 'additionally signifies time' (Latin *consignificatio*). A name is essentially a subject-expression (16ᵃ32 note), a verb is essentially a predicate-expression: 'it is a sign of things said of something else', 'it is always a sign of what holds, that is, holds of a subject'. Aristotle does not mean that a verb is the name of something that can be ascribed to something (as is 'running' or 'redness'), but that it is a sign that something *is* being ascribed to something ('runs', 'reddens'). Since he has in mind the simplest kinds of statement he fails to distinguish between the predicative and the assertive functions of 'runs'. In 'If Socrates runs, Callias walks', 'runs' performs a predicative but not an assertive function. The same is true of verbs in moods other than the indicative. Such phrases as 'a sign of things said of something else' blur this distinction, which is indeed easy to overlook if one concentrates exclusively on simple statements.

Aristotle does not raise the question whether it is necessary or only accidental that the two features distinguishing verbs from names should go together. Could there be a language in which the naming part of a sentence carried the time-reference while the saying or predicative part was 'without time'?

How would Aristotle analyse such sentences as 'Socrates hit Callias', 'Socrates is a man', 'Socrates is white'—where the saying part does not consist of a single word? He does, indeed, use such examples as 'Socrates is white' ('when "is" is predicated additionally as a third thing', 19^{b}19); but he does not state explicitly whether 'is' or 'is white' or 'white' is to count as the verb, nor justify any decision by reference to his official account of verbs in Chapter 3. The difficulty is that the various features of a verb like 'runs' are divided between 'is' and 'white': 'is' carries a time-reference, and is a sign that something is being said to hold, but 'white' is a sign of the thing being said to hold. So neither word by itself satisfies the requirements of Chapter 3. Yet 'is white' (like other many-worded predicative expressions) seems not to satisfy the requirement that no part of a verb should be significant separately (16^{b}6). The evidence as to how Aristotle would have dealt with this problem is inconclusive. At 16^{a}15 'white' is (presumably) given as an example of a verb, and at 20^{a}32 'not-just' is given as an indefinite verb; however, since the copula can be omitted in Greek it may be that these examples are to be thought of as '(is) white' and '(is) not-just'. At 20^{b}2 name and verb are said to be transposed in sentences whose word-by-word translation is 'is white man' and 'is man white'; here 'white' is treated as a verb. At 19^{b}21 Aristotle is uncertain how to characterise the 'is' in 'a man is just' ('a third component—whether name or verb—in the affirmation'). Immediately before, at 19^{b}13, he has explicitly said that 'is', &c., are verbs because they carry a time-reference—but there the 'is' was existential, so the problem of the copula (or in general of composite predicative expressions) did not present itself. Finally, Aristotle's remark at 21^{b}9 that to say that a man walks is no different from saying that a man is walking might suggest that he would regard 'is walking' or 'is white' as verbs, and 'walking' and 'white' as mere fragments of verbs. We can only conclude that Aristotle has not thought out how his account of verbs, tailor-made for such cases as 'runs', is to be applied to more complicated cases, where the saying or predicative part of the sentence does not consist of a single word. The root of the trouble is Aristotle's failure clearly to distinguish between grammatical and logical analysis.

16^{b}11. Aristotle's statement that indefinite verbs hold indifferently of anything whether existent or non-existent calls to mind *Categories* 13^{b}27–35, where it is said that if Socrates does not exist 'Socrates is not sick' is true. An indefinite verb, then, appears to be an expression consisting of negative particle and verb. But it does not seem helpful to call such an expression indefinite, for it is not a sign that something indefinite holds of something but a sign that something definite does not hold. It is noteworthy that at 19^{b}10, though Aristotle has just alluded to indefinite verbs, he says that every affirmation contains a name and a verb or an indefinite name and a verb, and that no affirmation or negation can be without a verb. He evidently realizes that in 'a man does not recover' the 'not' does not turn the verb into something indefinite, but turns the whole sentence into a negative one, one which denies something definite, not one which affirms something indefinite. 'Indefinite verb' is a misnomer; 'does not recover' is a sentence-fragment, containing an ordinary verb together with the negative particle that will make the sentence a negative one.

At 20^{a}31 Aristotle gives 'not just' as an example of an indefinite verb. Elsewhere in the chapter he distinguishes between the negation '. . . is not just' and the affirmation '. . . is not-just' (he does this by word-order, not by using a hyphen), and the context makes it probable that what he has in mind as an example of an indefinite verb at 20^{a}31 is in fact 'not-just'. In any case one might entertain the possibility that by 'indefinite verb' he means, not an expression which combines with a subject-term to make a negative sentence, but an expression which, combined with a subject-term, makes an affirmative sentence with a negative predicate (like 'Socrates is not-wise' at 20^{a}26). But if so Aristotle could not have said that an indefinite verb holds indifferently of anything whether existent or not; for if Socrates does not exist at all he cannot have even an indefinite characteristic. A further reason for rejecting the suggestion that indefinite verbs are expressions like 'is not-wise' is that, though such expressions can be distinguished from expressions like 'is not wise' by word-order, no such distinction can be drawn with the ordinary Greek verb such as Aristotle uses for examples in Chapter 3. The Greek which is rendered 'does not recover' and 'does not ail' is in fact 'not recovers' and 'not ails'. With such unanalysed verbs Aristotle has no way of drawing a distinction similar to that which he can draw between 'is not wise' and 'is not-wise' (by writing 'not is wise' or on the other hand 'is not wise'). It seems, therefore, that Aristotle's notion of the indefinite verb cannot be elucidated with the aid of his later distinction between 'is not wise' and 'is not-wise'.

16^b16. It is strange that Aristotle, having said that a verb is what additionally signifies time, should here deny that past and future tenses are verbs on the ground that they do not refer to present time. He draws the distinction again only at 17^a10; contrast $19^b10–14$. Had he wished to draw a distinction analogous to that between names and inflexions of names (16^a32) he could have done so; he could have said that a verb can combine with a name to yield a truth or falsehood, whereas an inflexion cannot. This would mark off the indicative mood from other moods (and from participles and infinitives). The distinction Aristotle in fact draws is not at all parallel to that between names and inflexions of names. He presumably regards the present tense as primary and the past and future as secondary because past time is time before now and future time time after now, so that references to past and future incorporate references to now (but not vice versa). The dispensability in Greek of the *present* tense of the copula may have encouraged the idea that the present is the standard tense of a verb and the past and future are deviations from it.

16^b19. This is a difficult passage. The gist of the first sentence is, however, clear enough: a verb on its own does not say that anything is the case, does not constitute a statement (cp. 16^a9, 17^a17). Aristotle must be using 'name' here in its wide, non-technical sense; he explains what he means by it by adding 'and signifies something'. He is not saying that 'runs' on its own is a name and not a verb, but he is bringing out that 'runs' needs a subject if it is to perform the assertive role for which it is cast. It is tempting to translate the last words of the sentence by 'whether anything is or is not the case'; and similarly at 16^b29 (instead of 'that it is or is not'). This gives the correct point but is probably an incorrect translation. The natural subject of the 'is' in the Greek is the previously mentioned 'thing' which the verb (or, at 16^b28, the name) signifies: 'runs' by itself does signify something, running, but not that that thing is, i.e. not that there is any running; only if you add a name ('Socrates runs') will you be saying that there is some running.

But how does the second sentence of the passage support the first? Some preliminary remarks: (a) Though Aristotle uses the infinitives 'to be' and 'not to be', these must—if the sentence is to have any relevance to what went before—be taken as stand-ins for indicative forms, 'is', 'is not', 'was', &c. (b) 'Nor if you say simply "that which is" ' seems to make a subsidiary point, and can best be put in brackets. (c) The word here (and elsewhere) translated by 'actual thing' applies to deeds, facts, states of affairs, &c., as well as to objects. Here 'fact' would be natural in English; statements state (or purport to state) facts, but an isolated name or verb does not.

Two alternative interpretations of the sentence now suggest themselves, corresponding to two alternative readings in line 22. One may read here either *ou* ('not') or *oude* ('not even'). With the former reading the translation would run: 'For "to be" or "not to be" is not a sign. . .'. How would this support the preceding statement? Perhaps Aristotle has in mind what he will say at 21^b9–10, that a verb like 'walks' is equivalent to 'is walking'. He would then be arguing along the following lines. We can show that no verb on its own constitutes as assertion if we can show that no expression of the form 'is walking' constitutes an assertion (since any verb can be put into this form). But anyone tempted to think that 'is walking' states something—says that something *is*—would be so tempted by the presence of 'is' in 'is walking'. In fact, however, this 'is' merely marks a combination or synthesis, a synthesis which cannot be grasped in thought without the elements synthesized. The 'is' in 'is walking' does not assert the existence of anything; it does not even signify anything in the way 'walking' does ('by itself it is nothing'); it is simply a sign of synthesis and can perform its function only in association with two proper terms. The 'is' in 'is walking' still awaits one of the two terms it is to link. Since all verbs can be put into the form of 'is walking' no verb constitutes a complete statement; it awaits the other component demanded by the copulative 'is'.

The objection to this interpretation is that it uses as a vital step in the argument a point not so much as hinted at here, and not made much of elsewhere, the point that 'walks' and so on are equivalent to 'is walking' and so on.

With the other reading, which has been adopted in the translation, a different interpretation imposes itself. Lines 22–25 do not now purport to prove the general point just made about verbs; rather they seek to dispose of a particular counter-example which somebody might raise against the general point. Somebody might suggest that though, say, 'walks' by itself does not say that anything is, yet surely 'is' does just that; if 'walks' does not assert existence, surely 'exists' does? No, says Aristotle: '*not even* "to be" or "not to be" is a sign of the fact.'

There remains the question how, with this reading and interpretation, the last part of the sentence is to be understood. (*a*) It may be taken (as on the first interpretation) as characterizing the copulative 'is'. So far from doing more than an ordinary verb—as somebody might suggest—'is' does less. It is merely a mark of synthesis. 'Walks' at least signifies something, but 'is' stands for nothing that can be thought of by itself ('by itself it is nothing'); it has no *significatio*, only *consignificatio*. ('Additionally signifies some combination' suggests that it also has some straightforward signification; but that Aristotle's expression need not imply this is shown by what he says at 20ᵃ13. 'So "every" and "no" additionally signify nothing other than that the affirmation or negation is about the name taken universally.' He does not, of course, mean that 'every' has some straightforward significance and *also* serves to quantify the subject, but that what its presence *adds* to a sentence is quantification.) If this is what Aristotle means, his remark is good in itself but weak as a rebuttal of the suggestion that 'is' *is* 'a sign of the fact'. For one who made this suggestion would be thinking of the existential 'is', and his suggestion would not be defeated by a remark about the copula. Aristotle may, however, easily have overlooked this, since he himself often seems to confuse or assimilate the existential and the copulative uses of 'to be'.

(*b*) Perhaps Aristotle's last remark is not about the copulative but about the existential 'is'. If so, 'by itself it is nothing' does not characterize the copula in contrast to ordinary verbs. It means only that 'is' ('exists'), *like* other verbs, *asserts* nothing on its own. Like them it both signifies something and also indicates a synthesis—it calls for the addition of a subject-term in order that it may fulfil its role as a sign of something said of something else.

So much must suffice to indicate the main possibilities of interpretation of this difficult passage. There remains for consideration the parenthesis 'nor if you say simply "that which is" '. Whereas in the preceding line Aristotle has used 'to be' and 'not to be' to represent 'is', 'is not', &c., this remark must be about the actual expression 'that which is'. The logical point involved seems to be quite different from the main point of the passage, though naturally connected with it. Roughly: someone might suggest that if 'is' does not make a statement because it does not say *what* is, then surely 'what is' ('that which is') does make a statement—surely 'what is' does say what is. Aristotle is, of course, right to reject this suggestion, but the reason has nothing to do with the verb 'to be' in particular; *no* substantival expression can state that something is the case.

CHAPTER 4

16^b26. The Greek word *logos*, here rendered by 'sentence', is the verbal noun from a verb whose primary meanings are 'count', 'tell', 'say', 'speak'. Short of simply transliterating it the translator is forced to adopt different renderings for it in different contexts. As Aristotle defines it at the beginning of this chapter it clearly covers both sentences and phrases, and this is its dominant meaning in this work. 'Sentence-or-phrase' is, however, a cumbrous expression, and in the translation a choice is made between 'sentence' and 'phrase' according to the context. The reader must remember that both are renderings of the one Greek word. Moreover, in some places neither 'sentence 'nor 'phrase' can serve to translate *logos*. It is translated by 'account' at 16^b1, 19^a28, $^b19$, 21^b24; by 'definition' at 17^a11, 21^a29; by 'statement' at 19^a33, 23^a28; by 'reason' and 'reasonable' at 21^b14, 22^a14; by 'rational' and 'rationally' at 22^b38-23^a4. In the *Categories* it has most often been rendered by 'definition', but by 'statement' at 4^a22, 12^b6-10, 14^b14-22, by 'language' at 4^b23, $^b32-35$, 5^a33-36, by 'talking' at 13^a24, by 'speech' at 14^a36, $^b2$.

Aristotle here gives the *minimum* requirements for a sentence-or-phrase. 'Some part'—and not 'every part'—because the letters of words and the syllables of polysyllabic words are parts of the sentence-or-phrase without being independently significant parts. On this and on 16^b28-33 see note on 16^a19. 'As an expression, not as an affirmation': Aristotle is not denying that a part of a sentence may be an affirmation (as in a conjunctive sentence), but only that it must be; he is concerned to give the minimal necessary conditions for being a sentence-or-phrase.

16^b33. 'Not as a tool but by convention': cp. 16^a19, $^a26$, note on 16^a3. See also Plato's *Cratylus* 386d–390e.

The translation 'statement-making sentence' must not be taken to imply that Aristotle draws the now familiar distinction between sentences (linguistic units which are neither true nor false) and statements

(which *are* true or false and which we make by using sentences). For
him a statement is just a sort of sentence, the sort that is true or false.
'Statement-making' simply represents the adjective from the noun
meaning 'statement' ('statemental' is hardly possible, while 'declara-
tory' and the like lose the identity of root which is apparent in the
Greek noun and adjective).

'Those in which there is truth or falsity': cp. *Categories* 2ª7 ('every
affirmation, it seems, is either true or false') and *De Interpretatione*
17ᵇ26–34. On singular statements about non-existent individuals
see *Categories* 13ᵇ27–33 (affirmations are false, negations true). Aristotle
does not explicitly discuss general statements involving empty classes
(though see 16ª16–18 on 'goat-stag'), but in his treatment of the
logical relations of quantified statements in Chapter 7 he may well
be assuming that (as with statements about individuals) the non-
existence of the subject-class makes affirmations false and negations
true. As for predictive statements, it *may* be Aristotle's view in
Chapter 9 that some of these lack a truth-value when they are made
but acquire one later; see notes there. Had Aristotle reflected further
on the puzzle he discusses at *Categories* 4ª22 ff. he might have been led
to a distinction such as that between sentences and statements, and
so to a more careful and sophisticated account of the relation of
sentences to truth and falsity.

CHAPTER 5

Aristotle has just said that this work deals with statements. But it
does not deal with all kinds of statement. In this chapter Aristotle
classifies statements and identifies the affirmation and the negation—
with which he is to be primarily concerned—as the two sorts of *simple*
statement. ('Negation' seems preferable to 'denial', though for the
corresponding verb it will be necessary to use 'deny'.) The chapter is
disjointed: 17ª9 and 17ª17 contain remarks irrelevant to the main
theme; the parenthesis at 17ª13 goes with what follows rather than
what precedes; 'these' in 17ª20 must refer right back to the single
statement-making sentences of 17ª15. The main questions that arise
are: (*a*) what is Aristotle's criterion for distinguishing what is one
statement from what is more than one? (*b*) what are his two types of
(single) statement? (*c*) how does he distinguish among simple statements between affirmations and negations?

(*a*) Aristotle does not give a general criterion for 'single statement'
and then differentiae to distinguish simple from compound single
statements. Instead he characterizes at once his two types of single

statement, that which 'reveals a single thing' (the simple) and that which 'is single in virtue of a connective' (the compound); and then gives two alternative grounds for counting an expression as more than one statement ('if more things than one are revealed or if connectives are lacking'). This is a disconcerting procedure. For if a statement can be single in virtue of a connective, surely the only way in which an expression could be more than one statement would be for it to consist of two or more single statements (whether simple or compound) lacking connectives to join them. On Aristotle's scheme a compound expression of a suitable sort would seem to qualify both as a single statement ('single in virtue of a connective') and as more than one statement ('if more things than one are revealed').

(b) It is pretty clear from Chapter 8 and the beginning of Chapter 11 what contrast Aristotle has in mind when he speaks of statements that reveal one thing and not many. He is not thinking of ambiguity, nor of grammatical form alone. He has in mind the fact that, in an unambiguous sentence of the form 'S is P', what 'S' stands for and what 'P' stands for may or may not be real genuine unities. This is nothing to do with whether 'S' and 'P' are single words or phrases. 'Callias is a two-footed land animal' is a simple statement and affirms one thing of one thing, because 'two-footed land animal' names one thing, a genuine single universal, a natural kind ($17^{a}13$). On the other hand, 'Callias is a cloak', supposing 'cloak' means 'white walking man', does not affirm one thing of one thing, because what 'cloak' stands for is not a genuine single universal or kind ($20^{b}18$). Aristotle does not tell us how to decide whether what a given expression stands for is genuinely one thing or universal or kind. His assumption that this is a decidable question corresponds to his assumption in the *Categories* that a 'What is *X*?' question permits only the answer which places *X* in *the* species or genus to which it belongs. The question which Aristotle postpones, at $17^{a}14$, to a different inquiry is discussed in the *Metaphysics* (Z 12, H 6 and I 9); but it is not easy to understand his answer, let alone to apply it in order to decide in individual cases whether what an expression stands for is or is not a genuine unity or real kind.

To return to the *De Interpretatione*, if a simple statement is one which predicates (affirms or denies) one thing of one thing, and a compound statement is one made up of simple statements joined together, what is to be said of 'Callias is a white walking man'? It is clearly the sort of sentence Aristotle has in view when he speaks of revealing many things; so it should count as more than one statement. Yet should it not also count as a single (compound) statement? One might, indeed, distinguish it from sentences containing connectives (and one might distinguish 'Callias is white and walking and a man' from sentences containing sentence-connectives). Yet one sees that such a sentence reveals many things by seeing that it is *equivalent* to the corresponding sentence containing sentence-connectives ('Callias is white and Callias is walking and Callias is a man'); compare 18ᵃ20–25. Thus, while there might be point in distinguishing overtly molecular sentences from covertly molecular ones, it seems odd if an overtly molecular sentence is to count as a single (compound) statement, while the equivalent covertly molecular one is to count as more than one statement. Aristotle ought either to have adopted a purely grammatical criterion (so that 'Callias is a white walking man' would have been one statement and not several), or to have relied on the notion of a single thing's being revealed (so that 'Callias is white and Callias is a man' would have been two statements and not one). He attempts to blend two criteria which are not of the same type, and he fails to make himself clear.

(c) Aristotle does not tell us how to decide whether a given simple statement is an affirmation or a negation. He would presumably rely on the presence or absence of a suitably-placed 'not'. This is perhaps why he says 'first . . . the affirmation, next . . . the negation': the negation presupposes, in that it involves adding something to, the affirmation. It is not clear, however, that any such purely grammatical or formal criterion ought to satisfy Aristotle. For the question whether a statement affirms or denies something of something would be for him the question whether the thought symbolized by the words is the thought of the things as joined or as disjoined (Chapter 1). Thus he is entitled to regard the presence of a suitably-placed 'not' as proof that a statement is a negative one, only if he can establish independently that all the *thoughts* expressed by such statements are negative (of things as disjoined). Aristotle does not, however, discuss how one would decide, with respect to a thought, whether it is affirmative (of things as joined) or negative (of things as disjoined). For the narrow range of cases he is to deal with, his simple linguistic criterion no doubt serves well enough.

17ᵃ17. That neither a name by itself nor a verb by itself can constitute a statement follows from Aristotle's definitions: a statement is a kind of *logos*, and a *logos* must, while a name or verb cannot, contain independently significant parts (Chapters 2–4). The question remains whether Aristotle's definition of 'statement' is either faithful

to ordinary Greek usage or philosophically useful. Consider the following cases. (*a*) In answer to the question 'Who is singing?' Callias says
'Socrates'. Has Callias not made a statement? He has not, of course,
stated that Socrates; but has he not, by saying just 'Socrates' in *this*
context, affirmed that Socrates is singing? (*b*) Callias says to Socrates
'you-are-singing', using no name or pronoun but simply the second
person singular of the verb. Has Callias not made a statement? It is
true that the utterance of 'you-are-singing' requires some context in
order that it may be the making of a statement; but it would seem
absurd to require that a separate personal pronoun be added in
Greek, and still more absurd to require that the name of the addressee
be used. (*c*) Callias says 'I-am-hungry' (first person singular of the
verb). Here the problem of reference that can arise with second or
third person verbs cannot arise. This utterance needs no special context in order to be the making of a statement (though there are, of
course, special contexts in which its utterance would not be the making
of a statement). Again it does not seem helpful to legislate that a
Greek speaker must throw in a separate personal pronoun or a name
if he is to qualify as having made a statement. The main points these
cases bring out are the desirability of distinguishing between a classification of sentences or other linguistic units and a classification of
speech-acts, and the necessity of studying the contextual requirements
that must be satisfied if utterances of various kinds are to qualify as
genuine statements, questions, orders, &c.

CHAPTER 6

Aristotle introduces now the idea of pairs of opposite statements, and
he examines various such pairs in Chapters 7 and 10. The argument
of 17^a26-31 seems rather pointless; perhaps Aristotle has in mind, and
wants explicitly to reject, the claim made by some previous thinkers
that false statement is impossible.

The term here translated 'contradiction' is elsewhere translated
'contradictory statements', 'contradictories', or the like. The word
translated 'opposite' is always so translated (and the corresponding
noun is translated 'opposition'). It will be found that Aristotle's
'contradictory statements' are not necessarily of different truth-values
(17^b29, 18^a10). It will also be noticed that he sometimes says 'opposite'
where the context shows that he means 'contradictory opposite' in
contrast to 'contrary opposite' (e.g. 17^b24, 20^a22).

The 'conditions' referred to at the end of the chapter will be designed to exclude such sophistries as that mentioned in *Sophistici Elenchi* 167ᵃ11 : an Ethiopian is black of skin but white of tooth, therefore he is black and he is not black.

CHAPTER 7

In this chapter Aristotle deals with four pairs of statements about universals, each pair consisting of an affirmation and a negation:

(*a*) 'every man is white' and 'no man is white';
(*b*) 'a man is white' and 'a man is not white';
(*c*) 'every man is white' and 'not every man is white';
(*d*) 'no man is white' and 'some man is white'.

He classifies the statements of (*a*) as contrary opposites, those of (*b*), (*c*), and (*d*) as contradictory opposites. He points out that not every contradictory pair consists of one true and one false statement: both statements of (*b*) may be true (17ᵇ29–33, 18ᵃ10). Contraries cannot both be true but their opposites (he means contradictory opposites) may (17ᵇ22–26).

It will be convenient in discussion to use the following traditional labels: 'every man is white' and 'no man is white' are universal statements (*A* and *E* respectively); 'some man is white' and 'not every man is white' are particular statements (*I* and *O* respectively); 'a man is white' and 'a man is not white' are indefinite statements.

It is a pity that Aristotle introduces indefinite statements at all. The peculiarity of the indefinite statement is that it lacks an explicit quantifier (there is no indefinite article in Greek and the word-for-word translation of Aristotle's sentence is 'man is white'; 'a man is white' seems, however, to come closer to the force of the Greek sentence). It may on occasion be intended universally ('what is being revealed may be contrary', 17ᵇ8). But since Aristotle does not exploit this, but treats indefinite statements as logically equivalent to *I* and *O* statements, he might as well have dispensed with them altogether and confined his attention to *A*, *E*, *I*, and *O* forms (cp. *Prior Analytics* 29ᵃ27).

Aristotle's concept of contradiction here is, of course, different from ours, in that he counts as contradictory the two statements of (*b*)—that is, in effect, *I* and *O* statements—which may be true together. This is not in itself an objection to Aristotle's procedure, but we are entitled to ask on what grounds he classifies (*b*) with (*c*) and (*d*) and distinguishes them all from (*a*). His own definition of a contradictory pair makes it to be an affirmation and negation which affirm and deny the same thing of the same thing (17^a33-35). What does 'of the same thing' mean in the case of quantified statements? One might rule that an affirmation and negation having the same predicate are '*of* the same thing' if and only if they are necessarily of different truth-values (i.e. they are contradictories in the modern sense of the word). But since Aristotle counts (*b*) statements as contradictory he is obviously not applying this rule. Alternatively one might require only that the affirmation and negation be about the same universal. But this, though it would make (*b*) statements contradictories, would also make (*a*) statements contradictory. It is thus not clear what interpretation of his own definition of contradiction ('the same thing of the same thing') entitles Aristotle to say that (*b*) statements are but (*a*) statements are not contradictories. There seems in fact as much reason to distinguish (*c*) and (*d*) from (*b*) as from (*a*). (*a*) and (*b*) share important characteristics which (*c*) and (*d*) lack: each of them consists of two statements which are similar in respect of quantification and which can have the same truth-value ('true' for (*b*), 'false' for (*a*)). Perhaps Aristotle is influenced by the fact that whereas the negative sentence in (*b*), as in (*c*), differs from the affirmative simply by the addition of 'not'—and the same is almost true in Greek of (*d*) also —this is conspicuously not so with (*a*).

At 17^b12-16 it is not clear whether Aristotle wishes to say that there cannot be a statement with universally quantified predicate, or that there cannot be a true statement of that kind. In *Prior Analytics* 43^b20 he says that such forms as 'every man is every animal' are 'useless and impossible'.

CHAPTER 8

18^a13. Aristotle did not require in Chapter 5 that a single statement should necessarily state only one thing (it might be single 'in virtue of a connective'); but he did require this of a *simple* single statement (which 'reveals one thing'). And he treated affirmations and negations as the two kinds of simple statement. The present account of single affirmations and negations therefore fits what was said in Chapter 5; and the argument that follows is not damaged by the fact that 'a horse is white and a man is white' is a single (compound) statement— it is not a simple statement and therefore not a single affirmation.

18^a18. We are to suppose that the name 'cloak' is given to horse and man, two things which do not 'make up one'. Aristotle indicates two ways in which 'a cloak is white' might be taken: firstly, as equivalent to 'a horse and a man is white', secondly, as equivalent to 'a horse-and-man is white'. But 'a horse and a man is white' is equivalent to 'a horse is white and a man is white', which clearly contains more than one affirmation; while 'a horse-and-man is white' signifies nothing, since nothing is a horse and a man. So on neither option is 'a cloak is white' one affirmation.

Though two interpretations of 'a cloak is white' are suggested, Aristotle is not discussing ambiguity of names. He is not saying that one who says 'a cloak is white' may mean 'a horse is white' and may mean 'a man is white'. A name given to two things that do not make up one is not an ambiguous name but an unambiguous name standing for what is not a genuine unity. See note (b) on Chapter 5, and the beginning of Chapter 11.

To say that 'cloak' stands for A and B does not say how sentences using 'cloak' are to be understood. The alternatives Aristotle considers are reasonable. Unfortunately his argument is vitiated by his choice of 'horse' and 'man' as values for 'A' and 'B'. For it is on the ground that nothing is both a horse and a man that he concludes that 'a cloak is white', understood in the second way, is not significant (and *a fortiori* not an affirmation). But a name that stands for two things which do not 'make up one thing' certainly need not be a name for two things that never go together. If one takes 'cloak' as equivalent to 'white walking man' Aristotle's way of disposing of the second way of construing 'a cloak is white' fails. Yet 'white walking man' is undoubtedly an example of an expression that does not—as 'two-footed land animal' does—stand for a genuine unity (17^a13, 20^b15–19; cp. *Metaphysics* Z 4). Thus Aristotle fails to show that if 'cloak' stands for two things and 'a cloak is white' is understood in the second way, it does not constitute a single affirmation. Nor could Aristotle, faced with this, retract and disallow the second way of interpreting 'a cloak is white'. For it is beyond question that actual words that stand for non-genuine unities are used very often in this way. 'Cobbler' does not stand for a genuine species; but 'all cobblers are kind' is certainly never used as equivalent to 'all men are kind and all who make shoes are kind', but always as equivalent to 'all shoe-making men are kind'. Similarly, 'some white walking men are tall' is obviously never used as equivalent to 'some white things are tall and some walking things are tall and some men are tall', but always in the second of the two ways indicated by Aristotle as ways of interpreting sentences involving 'cloak'.

It is, of course, very doubtful whether Aristotle is entitled to deny significance to 'a cloak is white', understood in the second way, even if 'cloak' stands for horse and man. The reason he gives—'because no man is a horse'—would seem to commit him to the over-strong thesis that no empty class can be significantly mentioned. Perhaps he is really relying on the fact that no man could *possibly* be a horse; but even this does not make it obvious that every sentence involving 'cloak' and understood in the second way is non-significant.

At the end of the chapter Aristotle infers that 'it is not necessary, with these statements either, for one contradictory to be true and the other false'. That this necessity does not hold for 'a cloak is white' follows already from the fact that it is indefinite. But by 'these statements' Aristotle means *any* statements involving 'cloak'-words. If 'some cloak is white' means 'some horse is white and some man is white', 'no cloak is white' means 'no horse is white and no man is white'; but then both contradictories ('some cloak is white' and 'no cloak is white') may be false—if, for example, no horse is white but some man is white. If, on the other hand, 'some cloak is white' is taken in the second way, it is, according to Aristotle, non-significant, and then neither it nor its contradictory is either true or false.

CHAPTER 9

This chapter has provoked vigorous discussion ever since it was written and not least in the last few years. Aristotle's brevity and lack of sophisticated technical vocabulary make it difficult to decide what he is maintaining. It is not possible here to attempt a full-scale interpretation of the chapter, let alone to report and discuss the many different accounts that have been given of it. The following notes aim only at opening up some of the difficulties and indicating some possible lines of thought.

The chapter falls into three parts. In Part I (18^a28-34) Aristotle says that a certain thesis does *not* hold of contradictory statements about particulars in the future (it will be convenient to call such statements 'future singulars'). In Part II (18^a34-19^a6) he develops an argument to show that if that thesis did hold of future singulars then everything that happens would happen of necessity (a consequence which we may conveniently label 'determinism'). In Part III (19^a7-$^b4$) Aristotle denies that everything that happens happens of necessity, and he states his own view about future singulars.

It is appropriate to say something at once about Aristotle's use of 'necessary', 'of necessity', and 'necessarily'. First, we must recognize the possibility that he fails to distinguish between the 'necessarily' which modifies a proposition and the 'necessarily' which marks the necessary *connexion* between a protasis and apodosis (or between premisses and conclusion). In his treatment of modal logic in *Prior Analytics* Aristotle seems to be reasonably clear about this distinction, although he uses modes of expression that are potentially misleading. It is perfectly possible that in the present chapter he is guilty of confusion on the point. Next, Aristotle does not, here or in other works, draw a sharp distinction between logical and causal necessity; he treats laws of logic and laws of nature as on a par. Moreover he appears, at least in this chapter, to use 'necessity' to cover what may be called *temporal* necessity—the unalterability of whatever has already happened. It may be that some of the obscurity in the chapter is due to his failure explicitly to distinguish these different types of necessity.

As a final preliminary to comment on the text let us state in rough terms two radically different overall interpretations that have found favour at various times. (1) The thesis introduced and denied by Aristotle at the beginning of the chapter is and is known by him to be ambiguous. It might be the strong thesis (*a*) : of any two contradictories one is necessarily true and one is necessarily false; that is, in effect, either necessarily-*p* or necessarily-not-*p*. Or it might be the weak thesis (*b*) : of any two contradictories necessarily one is true and one is false; that is, in effect, necessarily either *p* or not-*p*. Aristotle denies (*a*), which entails determinism, but accepts (*b*), which does not. (2) Aristotle's discussion does not turn on the above ambiguity. The thesis he introduces and denies is (*b*). He accepts as valid the argument in Part II which purports to show that (*b*) entails determinism, and he rejects (*b*). He does, however, hold that a thesis rather similar to (*b*) is true of future singulars, the thesis that of two such contradictories it is necessary that one should *at some time* be true and one false.

The gist of (1) is the distinction between 'necessarily (*p* or not-*p*)' and 'necessarily *p* or necessarily not-*p*'. The gist of (2) is the distinction between 'necessarily (*p* is true or not-*p* is true)' and 'necessarily (*p* will be true or not-*p* will be true)'.

18ª28. It is essential to look closely at these lines in order to decide what Aristotle means when he says at 18ª33 that with future singulars 'it is different'. In these lines he uses two rather similar phrases: 'necessary for the affirmation or the negation to be true or false' and 'necessary for one to be true and the other false'. It is clear that a different meaning must be attached to each of these. For Aristotle first says something about all statements concerning what is and what has been, and then draws a distinction within that class of statements. So what he asserts of *all* such statements cannot be the same as what he proceeds to assert as holding of only *some* such statements. Now there is no doubt what distinction he is drawing (see 17^{b}26–33): some pairs of contradictories must consist of one true and one false, others need not—both contradictories may be true. But then 'necessary for the affirmation or the negation to be true or false' must mean something weaker than 'necessary for one to be true and the other false', something that holds of all statements about what is and what has been even though 'necessary for one to be true and the other false' does not hold of all such statements. The phrase must then surely mean 'necessary that the affirmation (and equally that the negation) should be either true or false'. This would in any case be the most natural way to take the phrase; and it is the way in which any careful reader must understand it here. (It is true that Aristotle elsewhere uses similar phrases to express the idea that one contradictory must be true, one false. Thus at 17^{b}27 and 18^{a}10 this is what he means by 'necessary for one or the other to be true or false' and 'contradictory pairs are true or false'. But the contexts there make it quite clear how the phrases are intended there, just as the context at the beginning of Chapter 9 makes it clear that here 'necessary for the affirmation or the negation to be true or false' does *not* mean 'necessary for one to be true and one false'.) So Aristotle is saying in this paragraph: with statements about what is and what has been, each member of a contradictory pair is either true or false (with universal and singular statements the members must have different truth-values, but with 'indefinites' this is not so); but with future singulars it is different. Thus he is denying that it holds of future singulars that each of a contradictory pair must be either true or false.

18^{a}34. For if, Aristotle continues,[1] *every* affirmation or negation is

[1] The text translated and discussed is that of the best and most recent edition. There are, however, in this passage some quite well supported variant readings which should be mentioned. Their adoption would permit or even require a significantly different interpretation of the passage. Possible variant readings are as follows: ^{a}34 for 'if every affirmation or negation' read 'if every affirmation and negation'; ^{a}35 for 'everything either to be the case' read 'everything to be the case' and for 'For if one person says' read 'So if one person says'; ^{a}37 for 'if every affirmation is true or false' read 'if every affirmation or negation is true or false' or conceivably 'if every

true or false, everything must necessarily be the case or not be the case. This apodosis expresses the determinist conclusion which is later expanded and finally (19^a7) rejected. Aristotle's immediate task is to justify the implication just stated. First (18^a35-^b4) he argues that if every affirmation and negation has a truth-value it follows that of a contradictory pair about a future particular *either* the affirmation *or* the negation is true; if p is a future singular 'p is either true or false and not-p is either true or false' implies 'either p is true and not-p is false or p is false and not-p is true'. Aristotle then (18^b5 ff.) argues that the truth of whichever of the pair is true makes necessary the occurrence of the event truly forecast to occur (or the non-occurrence of the event truly forecast not to occur).

First, then, at 18^a35 Aristotle asserts that with contradictory future singulars necessarily just one is true—*if* every affirmation and negation is true or false. He then defends this against the suggestion that both might be true, saying that 'both will not be the case together under such circumstances'. 'Under such circumstances' contrasts the type of statement under consideration (contradictory future singulars) with a different type, already mentioned, for which the principle 'every affirmation and negation has a truth value' does *not* imply 'just one of a contradictory pair is true'—that is, statements about universals not taken universally. Aristotle supports the assertion that contradictory future singulars cannot both be true by drawing attention to the relation between the truth and falsity of statements and the actual occurrence and non-occurrence of events, &c. ('For if it is true to say . . .') He is assuming that the sea-battle cannot, of course, actually both happen and not happen, and he is inferring, given the relation of truth to fact, that the statements that it will happen and that it will not happen cannot both be true. He does not here deal with the possibility that both contradictories might be *false* (but see 18^b17-25). Perhaps he thinks that the reason he gives why contradictory future singulars cannot both be true serves also and obviously as a reason why they cannot both be false. Or perhaps he deals only with the suggestion that they might both be true because he has already allowed that two contradictories may both be *true* (if they are about universals not taken universally), and so might seem specially vulnerable to this suggestion in the case of future singulars also.

At 18^b4 Aristotle says: 'So it is necessary for the affirmation or the affirmation and negation is true or false'; $^b4$ for 'it is necessary for the affirmation or the negation to be true' read 'it is necessary for the affirmation or the negation to be true or false'.

negation to be true.' He means, of course, that it is necessary on the supposition that every affirmation and negation is true or false. Here and in what follows he puts himself in the place of the determinist and argues that determinism does indeed follow from that supposition. $18^b5–9$: since either the affirmation or the negation is true everything happens and will happen of necessity and never as chance has it. 'Since either he who says . . .' repeats the proposition just arrived at— 'it is necessary for the affirmation or the negation to be true'.

The phrase translated 'as chance has it' has been variously rendered by 'random(ly)', 'as the case may be', 'whichever happens', 'fortuitous(ly)', 'indeterminate(ly)'. Aristotle sometimes speaks as though 'of necessity' and 'not by chance' are equivalent. In fact, however, he distinguishes, among things that do not necessarily and always happen in one way, between those that usually and as a rule happen one way rather than the other, and those that do not have any such tendency to turn out one way rather than the other. It is to the latter type of non-necessary cases that the phrase 'as chance has it' applies. See 18^b8 ('what is as chance has it is no more thus than not thus'), 19^a20 ('with other things it is one rather than the other and as a rule'), 19^a19 ('of the affirmation and the negation neither is true rather than the other'), 19^a38 ('or for one to be true rather than the other'). The distinction between what happens as a rule, though not always, and what happens by chance is found elsewhere in Aristotle, e.g. at *Physics* $196^b10–17$. It does not seem to play an essential role in the present chapter, and indeed it fits very awkwardly into it. For the distinction is between *kinds* of event, and the determinist of this chapter is neither asserting nor denying that every event is of a kind that always happens. He could well allow that many events are of a kind that only usually happen or only happen as often as not, and he could still use his arguments to show that whatever does happen happens necessarily. His arguments do not presuppose a principle of universal causation but rely on purely logical moves.

It will be noticed that in the last two of the passages quoted above Aristotle speaks not of things or events but of statements. What does he mean by saying that of two contradictory statements one may be true *rather* than the other? Suppose that old men are usually bald. Aristotle would presumably say that the statement 'the next old man we meet will be bald' is true rather than false. Would he mean simply that most individual statements to that effect are true or would he mean that any individual statement to that effect is more likely to be true than false?

The only support Aristotle gives for the highly dubious inference of 18^b5-9 is to be found in the phrases used at $18^a39-{}^b1$ and later at 18^b11-15: 'if it is true to say that it is white . . , it is necessary for it to be white'; 'But if it was always true to say. . . . Everything that will be, therefore, happens necessarily'. It is debatable whether Aristotle anywhere makes clear the flaw in this argument from truth to necessity.

18^b9. It has already been asserted that what is truly predicted cannot but occur. The determinist now adds that, whatever occurs, it was true to predict that it would occur; so that whatever occurs cannot but occur. He points out later, at 18^b33-19^a6, that the force of this does not depend on the assumption that a true prediction was in fact made but only that it could have been.

18^b17. The suggestion here rebutted, that both of two contradictory future singulars may be false, seems properly to belong in the section $18^a34-{}^b4$; see note there. The suggestion is seeking to evade the inference from 'every affirmation and every negation is true or false' to 'of every contradictory pair *either* the affirmation *or* the negation is true'. Aristotle's first argument (18^b18) simply begs the question; for the suggestion in hand is precisely that when the affirmation is false the negation need not be true. The second argument (18^b20) is not so much against the suggestion 'both false' as against this considered as an escape from determinism: if, inconceivably, both were false, the argument from truth to necessity (falsity to impossibility) would still hold, and it would be necessary for the event both not to happen and not not to happen.

18^b26. The first sentence is puzzling. What does 'these' refer to? Probably the last part of the sentence is to be understood not as part of the thesis from which absurdities follow, but as a summary of the absurdities which follow from the thesis contained in the lines 'if it is necessary . . . and the other false'; if so, the 'and' in 'and that nothing of what happens' has the force of 'viz' or 'I mean'.

19^a7. On 'this kind of possibility' (19^a17) compare 21^b12-17 and 22^b36-23^a11.

19^a23. This immensely difficult section divides into two. First ($^a23-32$) Aristotle talks of things and events, then ($^a32-39$) he draws corresponding conclusions concerning statements ('since statements are true according to how things are'). This dichotomy is slightly blurred by his use of the term 'contradictories' within the first part (at ᵃ27); but it is clear from what follows it that he is still here speaking of things or events and not yet of statements. 'The same account holds for contradictories' simply marks the transition from talk about necessary being or necessary not-being, taken separately, to talk about the necessity of being or not-being, considered together. Thus the first part of the paragraph itself falls into two sub-sections, which are presented as making essentially the same point ('the same account holds'). What exactly is this point? In the first sub-section Aristotle draws attention to the illegitimacy of dropping a qualification or condition—of passing from '. . . is of necessity when it is' to '. . . is of necessity'. In the second sub-section he warns against drawing an improper inference from 'it is necessary for X to occur or not to occur'. It is natural to suppose that he is warning against an inference to 'it is necessary for X to occur or it is necessary for X not to occur'. Yet surely the fallacy in this inference is *not* the same as that illustrated in the first sub-section. It looks as though Aristotle is confused. When he says 'one cannot divide and say that one or the other is necessary' he probably means that one cannot go from 'it is necessary for X to occur or not to occur' to 'it is necessary for X to occur' or to 'it is necessary for X not to occur'. For either of these illegitimate moves could reasonably be described as 'dividing', and since each involves leaving out something of the original formula they do represent the same sort of fallacy as that of the first sub-section. On the other hand, neither of these is a move that anyone (in Chapter 9 or elsewhere) is tempted to make; whereas the move to 'it is necessary for X to occur or it is necessary for X not to occur' is seriously tempting—and according to some it is *the* move Aristotle wishes in this chapter to show up as wrong. Perhaps, therefore, Aristotle is supposing that in rejecting inference from 'necessarily: X or not-X' to 'necessarily X' or to 'necessarily not-X' he is thereby rejecting inference from 'necessarily: X or not-X' to 'necessarily X or necessarily not-X'. It is not difficult to believe that Aristotle may have made this mistake, assisted by the ambiguity of 'cannot . . . say that one or the other is necessary'. Some such hypothesis seems required if we wish *both* to understand him as intending to forbid inference from 'necessarily: X or not-X' to 'necessarily X or necessarily not-X' *and* to give weight to the words 'the same account holds for contradictories'.

Final comment on this chapter can conveniently be given in the form of remarks about the two main lines of interpretation mentioned at the beginning.

(1) According to the first interpretation Aristotle holds that with some future singulars (those where both possibilities are open), though it is necessary that either p is true or not-p is true, it is neither necessary that p is true nor necessary that not-p is true. In saying that it is not necessary that p is true Aristotle does not mean what we should mean if we said that a proposition is not a necessary truth but a contingent one. For he would say that it *is* necessary that p is true if the present state of affairs makes it certain that the p-event will occur, or again if the p-event has already occurred. His '. . . is necessary' means something like '. . . is ineluctably settled'. The truth-value of all statements about the past is ineluctably settled, though we may not know in which way. But the truth-value of some statements about the future is not ineluctably settled—though it is settled and in the nature of things that either the affirmation or the negation is true. To say that a statement about the future is true is only to say that the thing will happen; to say that it is necessarily true is to say that the present state of affairs guarantees that it will happen. Some true predictions are necessarily true—if, that is, nothing done or occurring hereafter could make a difference; some are not necessarily true until the time when the predicted event occurs (when they forthwith become necessary); some are not necessarily true at first but become so before the time of the event—if, that is, things happen which make the predicted event inevitable. On this view a statement cannot first lack and then acquire a truth-value; truth is a timeless property. But a statement can first lack a 'necessity-value'—it can be at a certain time neither necessary nor impossible—and later acquire one. Future singulars in cases where both possibilities are open *are* neither necessary nor impossible, but they will become necessary or impossible in due course, at the latest when the predicted event occurs or fails to occur.

Whatever the obscurities and difficulties in a view such as this, it undoubtedly has some plausibility as an interpretation of this chapter. For Aristotle is certainly operating here with a somewhat peculiar conception of necessity; and much of what he says in Part III lends colour to the suggested interpretation. On the other hand: (a) on this account Aristotle does not end by establishing the denial with which (it was argued above) he starts. He starts by denying that every affirmation and every negation has a truth-value, but he ends by asserting this, though denying that every affirmation and negation has a necessity-value. (b) So far from defeating the determinist's plausible argument from a statement's being true to an event's being necessary, the solution suggested says nothing whatsoever to meet it.

The determinist in Part II does not argue from 'necessarily p or necessarily not-p'. He argues *to* this strong thesis, and hence to determinism, from the weak thesis 'necessarily: either p is true or not-p is true', claiming that if p is true the p-event cannot fail to occur. On the first interpretation Aristotle's answer does not meet the determinist's argument; it simply denies an implication he claims to prove. (c) Nor does it help to suggest that the opening thesis about future singulars is ambiguous. It has been argued above that, given the context, it is not ambiguous. But in any case the exposure of ambiguity in it would resolve the problem only if the development of the puzzle in Part II had exploited the strong (and false) version of the thesis, that is, 'necessarily p or necessarily not-p'. But it does not do so. Thus the solution on the first interpretation neither disputes the determinist's starting-point (that every affirmation and every negation is either true or false) nor refutes the argument from truth to necessity which he bases upon it.

(2) According to this interpretation Aristotle holds that a statement with a truth-value automatically has a necessity-value (if true, necessary; if false, impossible), but he claims that a statement may lack a truth-value and acquire one later. If this is Aristotle's solution the chapter hangs together well. For on this account what Aristotle denies at the beginning—that every statement is true or false—he denies also at the end, though he does allow that every statement is *at some time* true or false. The reason the determinist's argument from truth to necessity in Part II does not get refuted is that Aristotle accepts it as valid. He accepts the claim that if p is true the p-event cannot but occur, but he denies—what the determinist simply *assumed*—that it holds for all future singulars as for other statements that either the affirmation or the negation *is* true. He agrees that true statements mirror facts; but instead of accepting that since every statement is true or false all the facts are already there to be mirrored, he argues that since many future events are not yet determined statements about such events are not yet true or false—though in due course they certainly will be. Part III contains this argument, the 'since' clause being expounded in 19^a7–32 and the inference about statements being drawn in 19^a32–$^b4$.

This interpretation, then, makes the whole chapter fit together well. Nor, whatever we may think of it, does the suggested solution seem alien to Aristotle's way of thinking about truth. He seems to hold a rather crude realistic correspondence theory of truth, and we might well expect him to think that if the state of affairs now is such that it is not settled whether X will or will not occur, then 'X will occur' is not now either true or false: there is not yet anything in the facts for it to correspond or fail to correspond with. More specifically, the temporal words in the first section of Part III may be thought to favour this interpretation. Aristotle says that whatever occurs occurs necessarily *when* it occurs (but not: occurs necessarily). The corresponding statement about statements would be that whatever is true is necessarily true *when* it is true (but not: is necessarily true). This seems to open the door to the second interpretation. Unfortunately, the 'already' at 19^a39 is not as strong evidence as it appears; though the Greek adverb usually has a temporal sense, it can be used with a purely logical force, so that 'not already' means 'not thereby' or 'that is not to say that . . .'.

Two qualifications must be made to what has been said in favour of the second interpretation. (*a*) It is not quite accurate to say that on this interpretation what Aristotle denies at the beginning he denies at the end. For what he denies at the beginning is that every affirmation and negation is true or false, whereas what he denies at the end (19^b1–2, cp. 18^b29) is that of every affirmation and opposite negation one is true and one false. However, since the obnoxious consequences are mostly drawn from 'one true, one false', it is not unnatural that Aristotle should state his conclusion as the denial of that thesis (as applied to future singulars) and not as the denial of the thesis 'both have truth-values'. He has argued at 18^a35–$^b4$ that 'both have truth-values' entails, for future singulars, 'one true, one false', and he finds no fault with this argument So when in conclusion he denies the thesis 'one true, one false' he is by implication reaffirming his denial of the thesis 'both have truth-values'. He fails to take the final step that would round off the chapter, but it is easy to see that it can be taken. (*b*) It has been said that Aristotle accepts the argument of Part II as valid. This must not be taken to suggest that, on the second interpretation, he would be willing to use all the determinist's arguments. He could obviously, on this view, not assert, with the determinist: 'if it is white now it was true to say earlier that it would be white; so that it was always true to say of anything that has happened that it would be so' (18^b9–11). He could, however, allow that this is a true implication on the assumption that every statement has a truth-value; if the earlier prediction that it would be white had a truth-value it was without a doubt true and not false. So even here Aristotle can accept the validity of the determinist's argument, given his initial assumption. The rebuttal of the determinist depends on rejecting his assumption, not attacking his logic.

It must be admitted that a good deal of sympathy is needed if the second interpretation is to be given to the closing remarks of the chapter. Aristotle certainly does not state explicitly that his solution is that future singulars may be *now* neither true nor false though they will necessarily acquire a truth-value at some time. Thus, for example, at 19ᵃ36-38 he does not say that it is necessary for one of the two contradictories to be true and one false at some time though not already. He says: 'it is necessary for one or the other of the contradictories to be true or false—not, however, this one or that one, but as chance has it.' This is not absolutely fatal to the second interpretation. Even on this interpretation there is some point in 'not, however, this one or that one' (even though a temporal phrase like 'not, however, already' would be more welcome). For on this interpretation Aristotle allows only that it is necessary for one of the two contradictories to be true *at some time*. But if it were necessary for *this one* to be true at some time, it would follow (the matter being already settled) that this one was already true. So 'not this one or that one' can be taken as an indirect way of saying 'neither is *yet* true'. But evidently it is only if one is strongly predisposed in favour of the second interpretation that one will succeed in finding it expressed in 19ᵃ36-38. The statement at 19ᵇ1 is equally devoid of explicit reference to a type (2) solution: 'it is not necessary that of every affirmation and opposite negation one should be true and the other false.' This again is amenable to a type (2) interpretation, but it is certainly not in itself evidence in favour of such an interpretation of the chapter.

CHAPTER 10

The first part of the chapter is mainly concerned to distinguish different pairs of contradictory opposites according to whether there is or is not a copula (an 'is' which is 'predicated additionally as a third thing', 19ᵇ19) and whether terms are or are not negative. Thus:

| I | (a) | a man is (= exists) | a man is not |
| | (b) | a not-man is | a not-man is not |

II	(a)	(1) a man is just	a man is not just
		(2) a man is not-just	a man is not not-just
	(b)	(1) a not-man is just	a not-man is not just
		(2) a not-man is not-just	a not-man is not not-just

Verbs like 'walks' yield the same two possibilities, I (a) and (b), as does 'is' ('exists'). Each of the six possibilities may, of course, be exemplified by quantified contradictories, and Aristotle gives some such examples. The second part of the chapter (20^a16-40) contains remarks on the logical relations holding between various statements, together with a footnote on indefinite terms (20^a31–36). Finally (20^b1–12), Aristotle argues that transposing name and verb does not alter significance.

19^b5. Some references to this paragraph will be found in the notes on 16^a29 and on Chapter 3.

19^b19. 'There are two ways of expressing opposition': because what follows the 'is' (or 'is not') may or may not be a negative term— hence the subdivision of II (a) and II (b) above.

'Two of which will be related, as to order of sequence . . .': some help in interpreting this obscure remark can be derived from *Prior Analytics* I 46 (though the reference to the *Analytics* at 19^b31 is probably a later addition to the text of the *De Interpretatione*, whether put in by Aristotle or by an editor). Aristotle seems to have a diagram such as this in mind:

(*a*) a man is just	(*b*) a man is not just
(*d*) a man is not not-just	(*c*) a man is not-just
(*f*) a man is not unjust	(*e*) a man is unjust

He is saying that of the four statements (*a*)–(*d*): (*d*) is logically related to the affirmation in its column, (*a*), as (*f*) is; and (*c*) is related to the negation in its column, (*b*), as (*e*) is; but (*a*) is not related to (*d*) as (*f*) is, and (*b*) is not related to (*c*) as (*e*) is.

This is all straightforward if Aristotle means 'not-just' to be equivalent to 'unjust', as in the *Analytics* he treats 'not-equal' as equivalent to 'unequal'. However, while a number must be either equal or unequal to another Aristotle recognizes that there is an intermediate condition between justice and injustice (*Categories* 11^b38–12^a25). This would suggest the possibility that by 'not-just' he means (not 'unjust', but) 'either unjust or in the middle condition between being just and being unjust'. Correspondingly, 'not-white' would mean (not 'black', but) 'of some colour other than white'. It would still hold that 'is not just' does not entail 'is not-just' (stones are not just but they are not not-just), and there would be a good reason for Aristotle's mention of privatives like 'unjust', since 'is unjust', *like* 'is not-just', is *not* entailed by 'is not just'. On this view, however, the statement that (*d*) and (*f*) are identically related to (*a*), and (*c*) and (*e*) identically related to (*b*), is an over-statement. It is difficult to decide between the two suggestions as to precisely what force Aristotle means to attach to 'is not-just'.

In any event Aristotle is clearly distinguishing between 'is not just' and 'is not-just'. It is therefore surprising that at 20ᵃ23-26 he allows an inference from 'Socrates is not wise' to 'Socrates is not-wise', and that at 20ᵃ39 he throws out the remark that 'every not-man is not-just' signifies the same as 'no not-man is just'. (Cp. 20ᵃ30, where he describes 'every man is not-wise' as contrary to 'every man is wise' —that is, he treats it as equivalent to 'no man is wise'.) On either view about 'is not-just' 'X is not just' will not entail 'X is not-just' and 'no X is just' will not entail 'every X is not-just'. In the first case Aristotle is perhaps influenced by the actual subject term he uses in the example; Socrates, a man, is either wise or unwise or in the middle condition. There is no such excuse for the statement at 20ᵃ39.

19ᵇ36. 'These last are a group on their own': no statement with 'not-man' as subject implies or is implied by a statement with 'man' as subject. Statements with 'not-just' as predicate are not, in this sense, a group on their own, since such statements may imply or be implied by statements with 'just' as predicate.

20ᵃ3. 'Here one must not say . . .': if, that is, one wants (c) and (d) to differ from (a) and (b) just in having an indefinite name for subject, so that the quartet shall correspond to the quartet with 'is' as verb (19ᵇ17-19).

In the English there is a dissimilarity between these quartets: in the earlier one we have 'is' and 'is not' whereas in this one we have 'walks' and '*does* not *walk*'. But there is no such dissimilarity in the Greek. The phrase rendered by 'does not walk' is of the same form as that rendered by 'is not'. It differs from 'walks' only by the addition of the negative particle.

20ᵃ16. On the inference to 'Socrates is not-wise' see the end of note on 19ᵇ19. A further objection to this inference might be derived from *Categories* 13ᵇ15-35, which seems to imply that when Socrates did not exist 'Socrates is not wise' would be true but the affirmation 'Socrates is not-wise' would be false.

'With universals, on the other hand . . .': Aristotle explicitly denies that 'not every man is wise' entails 'every man is not-wise'. Does he mean also to deny that 'no man is wise' entails 'some man is not-wise' and that 'a man is not wise' entails 'a man is not-wise'?

20ᵃ31. See note on 16ᵇ11.

20^b1. It has been seen earlier in the chapter that the meaning of a sentence may be altered if a 'not' is moved from one place in it to another. Aristotle now considers a different type of change in word-order. His proof that 'a man is white' means the same as 'white is a man' rests partly on the principle that one affirmation has just one negation (17^b37–39), but also on the assertion that 'white is not a man' contradicts 'a man is white'. But this is in effect to assume that 'white is not a man' means the same as 'a man is not white'; and this would obviously not be admitted by anyone disposed to hold that 'a man is white' does not mean the same as 'white is a man'. So Aristotle's proof is not cogent.

Aristotle does not make clear here what in general would count as transposing the name and the verb in a sentence. Nor is his account of names and verbs elsewhere sufficiently clear and comprehensive to enable one to say whether he is justified in claiming that no such transposition affects significance.

CHAPTER 11

20^b12. The question what constitutes a single affirmation or negation has already been discussed in Chapters 5 and 8. Aristotle's treatment of the question is clearly unsatisfactory. He fails to recognize that a statement which contains a name (or verb) which does not stand for a genuine unity may nevertheless be itself a unitary statement, incapable of decomposition into simpler statements. 'Some men are musical cobblers' and 'no musical cobblers are wise' cannot be construed as conjunctions of simpler statements containing no such compound terms as 'musical cobblers'.

On dialectical questions and answers see *Topics* VIII and *Sophistici Elenchi* 169^a7 ff., 175^b39 ff., 181^a36 ff. Consider the question: 'Are Callias and Cleon at home?' Aristotle holds that a negative answer implies that neither is at home, and that consequently the question does not necessarily permit of a 'yes' or 'no' answer. But (*a*) the negative answer can be construed simply as a disjunction (with non-exclusive 'or') of negations—'Callias is not at home or Cleon is not at home'. Then the question does permit of a straight 'yes' or 'no' answer. (*b*) Even if it is allowed that 'are Callias and Cleon at home?' normally presupposes that they are both in or both out, and that the answer 'no' inevitably accepts this presupposition, still expressions that do not stand for genuine unities do not necessarily import such presuppositions into questions or statements in which they occur. The answer 'no' to the question 'Are some men musical cobblers?' does not commit the answerer to the view that there are musical cobblers. (*c*) A question or statement which makes a presupposition cannot be construed as a mere conjunction of 'simple' questions or statements. Before asking 'are some red dogs fierce?' I ought perhaps to ask 'are some dogs red?' But 'are some red dogs fierce?' is not equivalent to the conjunction of 'are some dogs red?' with some other question of the same simple kind.

20^b31. In this paragraph Aristotle asks under what circumstances one can pass from the assertion of two predicates separately to the assertion of them together. He brings up two kinds of case where one cannot. One kind is where the predication of the compound would be absurd because pleonastic (20^b37–21^a3). He deals with such cases at the end of the next paragraph by the simple rule that where one predicate is contained in another the assertion of them as a single compound predicate is impermissible (21^a16-18). The second kind of case is where the conjoint predication of two predicates may be false though each can be truly predicated on its own (20^b33-36). He deals with such cases at 21^a7–16.

21^a7. The second and third sentences of this paragraph illustrate what is meant in the first sentence by 'either of the same thing or of one another'. The fourth sentence claims that the rule given in the first sentence enables us to reject the inference from 'is good and is a cobbler' to 'is a good cobbler' while accepting that from 'is two-footed and an animal' to 'is a two-footed animal'.

It is not clear that the type of case considered in the third sentence ('or of one another') is essential for Aristotle's account. For since the problem is about combining predicates, the question whether, in 'the white is musical', 'white' and 'musical' are 'one thing', is relevant only indirectly, in so far as the answer to it would decide whether 'white' and 'musical' if predicable of something separately are therefore predicable together; but Aristotle already purports to deal with this question directly in the second sentence.

If two predicates are predicated accidentally of the same thing then they will not be one; and this is why though some inferences to combined predicates are valid others are not. This, roughly, is Aristotle's position. The first point to note is that his example, in the fourth sentence, of a valid inference (from 'is two-footed and an animal' to 'is a two-footed animal') is a case of a very special kind. 'Two-footed' and 'animal' make up a genuine unity in a strong sense, 'two-footed' being a differentia of 'animal' and forming, with it, the definition of a real natural kind. See note (*b*) on Chapter 5. But it is not, of course, this kind of unity that is relevant to the present problem. When Aristotle says that two accidental predicates 'will not be one', he cannot mean just that they cannot constitute a genuine real unity like 'two-footed animal'. This would be relevant to the problem about passing from separate predicates to a compound predicate only if Aristotle held that whenever two predicates do *not* form such a unity it is always illegitimate to pass from their separate to their conjoint predication. But his own examples of permissible transitions include (quite properly) that from '*X* is white and a man' to '*X* is a white man' (20^{b}34–35). Yet 'white man' is an excellent example of what is *not* a real or natural unity like 'two-footed animal'. (It is explicitly used as such an example in *Metaphysics* Z 6; and though earlier in Chapter 11 (20^{b}18) Aristotle's example of terms that do not make a real unity is not 'white man' but 'white walking man', there is no reason to suppose that he adds 'walking' there because 'white man' by itself *would* be a genuine unity. He also gives a *three*-word example for what is a real unity, 'tame two-footed animal', but here again a two-word example would have done.) Thus Aristotle could have given 'white man' just as well as 'two-footed animal' as his example, at 21^{a}15, of permissible combination. When he says at 21^{a}9 that certain predicates will not be one, this means only that they will not necessarily be truly predicable jointly just because they are truly predicable separately. 'Will not be one' and 'are not one' in this paragraph refer back to 'say them as one' in 20^{b}34–35, not to the 'one' (real genuine unity) of such earlier passages as 17^{a}13 and 20^{b}16.

Aristotle's solution to his problem is certainly inadequate. For he simply contrasts cases where two predicates are both accidents of the same subject with cases where they are not, that is, with cases where one or the other predicate gives the essence of the subject, (answers the question 'What is it?'). But though all cases of the latter kind may be cases where the transition to a compound predicate is legitimate, clearly not all cases of the former kind are cases where the transition is illegitimate. If someone is a cobbler and 6 foot tall it does follow that he is a 6-foot-tall cobbler. The difference between this case and the case of the person who is good and a cobbler—but not necessarily a good cobbler—is left entirely unexplained by Aristotle.

It is worth now returning to the third sentence of the paragraph, about things said accidentally of one another. 'Accidentally' does not mean the same here as when 'white' and 'musical' are said to be accidentally predicated of a man. This last means that 'white' and 'musical' are accidents (not part of the essence) of a man; but 'the white is musical' is accidental predication not because 'musical' is an accident of 'white' but, precisely, because it is not: 'musical' attaches to 'white' only incidentally or indirectly, in that it is an accident of that of which 'white' is also an accident. An explicit recognition of this second sense of 'accidentally' might have helped Aristotle to do better with his problem. For the cases where the inference from 'X is A and B' to 'X is AB' is invalid are not the cases where A and B are accidents of X (the inference from 'X is 6 foot tall and a cobbler' is valid); but they are just those cases where in the combined predicate 'AB' one of the elements qualifies the other *directly* and qualifies the subject only *indirectly*. In 'X is a good cobbler' 'good' qualifies 'cobbler' directly, and X only indirectly, *qua* cobbler. To say this is not, of course, to solve Aristotle's problem, since no general rule has been given as to which predicates function, when combined with others, as 'good' does in 'good cobbler'. But at least the problem is correctly located: which predicates become, when combined with others, qualifiers of the others and no longer direct qualifiers of the subject?

21ª18. Aristotle now turns to the question when a compound predicate can legitimately be divided into two separate predicates. The discussion falls into two parts corresponding to the two parts of the preceding paragraph. The rule against dividing when the compound implies a contradiction (21ª21–23, 29–30) corresponds to the rule against combining when one predicate contains the other (21ª17–19); the rule concerning accidental predication at 21ª24–28, 30–31 corresponds to the remarks about accidental predication at 21ª7–16.

'Some opposite is contained from which a contradiction follows': 'dead', for example, is an opposite, the opposite of 'living'; when it is added to 'man' a contradiction results, since a man is by definition an animal, that is, a kind of living thing.

It is clear that the accidental predication of which Aristotle speaks in this paragraph is 'accidental' in the second of the two senses distinguished above; it is incidental or indirect predication. Aristotle's example is not a happy one. But when he says that in 'Homer is a poet' the 'is' is predicated accidentally of Homer ('because he is a poet, not in its own right') his point evidently is *not* that 'is' gives an accidental as opposed to essential property of Homer, but that it attaches to Homer only indirectly, qualifying him only *qua* poet. Similarly with 'good' in 'X is a good cobbler'. Thus Aristotle uses for the problem about dividing compound predicates the notion of indirect qualifiers which he failed to exploit properly in discussing the previous problem about combining separate predicates.

CHAPTER 12

This chapter and the next contain important first steps in modal logic. Chapter 12 inquires what negations contradict modal affirmations, Chapter 13 investigates the logical relations of statements of different modalities. Aristotle's more developed treatment of modal logic, including modal syllogisms, is in *Prior Analytics* I 3 and 8-22; and his fullest general discussion of possibility and potentiality is in *Metaphysics* Θ.

The word *dunaton* is normally translated 'possible'; but at 21^{b}13-14 and from 22^{b}34 to the end of Chapter 13 it is translated 'capable'. The word has an impersonal use, as in 'it is *dunaton* for something to walk'; here it can be rendered by 'possible'. But it can also be used in a different construction, for example, 'something is *dunaton* to walk'; here it must be translated 'capable'. It must be remembered that this difference of translation does not correspond to any difference in Aristotle's terminology. (The noun *dunamis* is rendered by 'possibility' at 19^{a}17 but by 'capability' in Chapter 13 and by 'capacity' in *Categories*, c. 8.)

Another of Aristotle's modal terms is *endechomenon*. He does not distinguish in meaning between this and *dunaton*, and elsewhere there is no objection to translating it by 'possible'. In the present chapters, however, where Aristotle uses it and *dunaton* as two different (though equivalent) modal terms, it requires a different translation. The traditional rendering 'contingent' is highly misleading. Here it is rendered by 'admissible', a word that has some connexion with the original force of the Greek word and that has the merit of not being a familiar technical term. The reader must take it as a mere synonym of 'possible'.

21^{a}38. The difficulty Aristotle encounters in determining the contradictories of modal statements is due to his dangerously elliptical forms of expression. There would have been no puzzle if he had written out his examples thus: (a) 'a man is white'; (b) 'it is possible for a man to be white'. Replacing 'is' by 'is not' produces the required negation in both cases. If the examples are put into the infinitive a question does arise: (a) 'to be a white man'; (b) 'to be possible to be a white man'; which 'to be' in (b) is to be replaced by 'not to be'?

Aristotle's actual formulation conceals this (clear) question and gives rise to perplexity because he leaves out the first 'to be' in (b). Analogy with (a) then demands that 'possible to be' be negated by 'possible not to be'.

The strange-seeming argument about the log at 21^b3-5 is proof that one must take the examples in the preceding lines to be infinitival phrases (and not understand Aristotle's infinitives as standing for indicative sentences). The statement 'of everything the affirmation or the negation holds' makes sense only if by 'affirmations' and 'negations' one means, not statements, but (roughly) predicates. 'To be a white man' or 'not to be a white man' (or, as we should more naturally put it, 'being a white man' or 'not being a white man') does hold of everything. But, as the log argument shows, the same cannot be said of 'to be a white man' and 'to be a not-white man'.

It must, however, be allowed that Aristotle may not always clearly distinguish talk of a statement's being true and talk of a predicate's being *true of* something. In the present passage he immediately goes on to give examples which are indicative sentences ('a man walks', &c.). And in the subsequent discussion it is not everywhere clear whether expressions like 'possible to be' stand for sentences ('it is possible for . . . to be') or for predicates (. . . is 'possible to be', i.e. 'capable of being').

'Capable *in this way*' (21^b14): see 22^b36 ff. It is hard to know how to translate the last lines of this paragraph (21^b30-32), and hard, with any translation, to be sure what he is saying at 21^b26-32 and how it fits with his remarks at the end of the chapter (22^a8-13). His general idea seems to be this: both 'a man is white' and 'a man is not white' are 'about' white and man—these are the 'subject things' or subject-matter; 'is' and 'is not' are additions which produce respectively an affirmation and a negation. Analogously, 'it is possible a man is white' and 'it is not possible a man is white' are both about a man's being white; 'it is possible' and 'it is not possible' are additions producing respectively an affirmation and a negation. The key point, for Chapter 12, is simply that to negate a modal affirmation one must leave the subordinate *clause*—(that) 'a man is white'—unchanged, just as one must, in order to negate a non-modal affirmation, leave the *terms*—'a man' and 'white'—unchanged, and must not offer, for example, 'a not-man is white' as the negation of 'a man is white'.

But what does Aristotle mean by saying that in non-modal cases 'to be' and 'not to be' *determine the true*? And how is this related to his later suggestion that 'true' and 'not true' must be added on to 'to be' and 'not to be', these being treated as subjects? Here again difficulty is caused by his failure to write out examples in full. But presumably the first statement is drawing attention to the *assertive* role of 'is' in 'a man is white' in contrast to the non-assertive role it has in 'it is possible that a man *is* white' (of course the *other* 'is' here *is* assertive—only Aristotle leaves it out). The later statement cannot be meant to insist that some addition—whether an ordinary modal, or 'true' or 'not true'—must always be made in order that an affirmation or negation may result; for clearly 'a man is white' is an affirmation. Aristotle is insisting only that *when* some such addition is made (turning what was a complete statement into a subordinate clause) then it is the quality (affirmative or negative) of the addition that determines whether the new statement is an affirmation or a negation, the subordinate clause remaining unchanged in the affirmation and the contradictory negation.

CHAPTER 13

22ª14. For convenience of reference the quadrants in the table have been numbered I–IV, and arabic numerals will refer to lines; thus 'II 3' refers to 'impossible to be'.

The table is later corrected by the transposition of I 4 and III 4 (22ᵇ10–28). What is wrong with it at present can best be brought out by distinguishing two senses of 'possible' which Aristotle himself explicitly distinguishes in the *Prior Analytics* (e.g. 25ª37–40, 32ª18–21). 'Possible' may be defined as equivalent to 'not impossible' (one-sided possibility), or it may be defined as equivalent to 'not impossible and not necessary' (two-sided possibility). It will be seen that the implications given in I and III of Aristotle's original table hold only if 'possible' stands for two-sided possibility, while those in II and IV hold only if 'possible' stands for one-sided possibility. By his later transposition of I 4 and III 4 Aristotle makes the whole table correct, 'possible' everywhere standing for one-sided possibility. He does not work out a table for two-sided possibility.

22ª32. 'Contradictorily but conversely': from the contradictories 'possible' and 'not possible' there follow the contradictories 'impossible' and 'not impossible'—but *not* respectively: the negative 'not impossible' follows from the affirmative 'possible', the affirmative from the negative.

22ª38. Aristotle first comments on a peculiarity of the adjacent fourth lines in the upper half of the table. I 4 and II 4 are not (as are

I 3 and II 3) contradictories. Their respective contradictories are separated from them, not adjacent: the contradictory of I 4 is at IV 4, of II 4 at III 4. 'It is contraries which follow': I 4 and II 4 are called contraries presumably because they display the maximum difference from one another; they differ both in quality of mode ('not necessary'—'necessary') and in quality of *dictum* ('to be'—'not to be').

The last part of this paragraph, from 'The reason why these do not follow in the same way', seems to be misplaced. For it does not explain the fact just mentioned, that I 4 and II 4 are not contradictories but contraries. It explains simply why in any quadrant the infinitive (*dictum*) must have a different quality in the last line from that which it has in the first three. This is a feature of the correct revised table which is precisely not a feature of the incorrect original table. In the original table the quality of *dictum* is the same throughout quadrant I and the same throughout quadrant III. Thus this passage (22^b3–10) properly belongs *after* the amendment of the original table, that is, after 22^b10–28. 'In the same way' means 'with the quality of the *dictum* unchanged'; 'in a contrary way' and 'conversely' mean 'with the quality of the *dictum* changed'.

22^b10. Aristotle argues that the original table leads to self-contradiction. When he claims that 'necessary' must imply 'possible' since otherwise it would have to imply 'not possible' he is, of course, misusing the principle of excluded middle; it would have been sufficient for him to say that otherwise 'necessary' would have to be *consistent with* 'not possible'. Given then that 'necessary' implies 'possible' the original I 4 is clearly wrong. Aristotle shows that it cannot be replaced by either II 4 or IV 4, but that replacement by III 4 solves the problem and at the same time gets rid of the peculiarity of the original table which was discussed at 22^a38–$^b3$.

22^b29. This paragraph is not clearly thought out. There is no question but that 'possible' (one-sided) does follow from 'necessary' and does not imply 'possible not . . .', while 'possible' (two-sided) does not follow from (but is inconsistent with) 'necessary' and does imply 'possible not . . .'. Aristotle fails to present the matter in this way. He distinguishes between capabilities which are of opposites and capabilities which are single-track, and between capabilities being exercised and capabilities not being exercised; and he concludes that 'since the universal follows from the particular, from being of necessity there follows capability of being—though not every sort'. This is not very illuminating. Nor is it clear how the distinction between capabilities of opposites and single-track capabilities is related to what follows. The words 'not even all those which are "capabilities" of the same kind' imply that all the capabilities just considered are all in *one* of the two types next to be distinguished. If so, since they include capabilities of opposites, they must be in the type exemplified by 'capable of walking because it *might* walk'. But does not Aristotle think that fire is always exercising its power of heating ('with everything else that is actualized all the time')? In any case fire's power to heat cannot go exclusively into the type consisting of merely dispositional powers, since it is certainly sometimes actualized. The truth is that this whole discussion is too compressed; the topics are more at home in the *Metaphysics* and are best studied there (in Book Θ, especially Chapters 1, 2, and 5).

23ᵃ21. This paragraph reeks of notions central to the *Metaphysics* but out of place in the present work and only tenuously connected with what preceded. It is safe to regard it as a later addition, whether by Aristotle or by another. On the priority of actuality cp. *Metaphysics* Θ 8. 'Primary substances' is used here, as in the *Metaphysics*, to refer to pure forms without matter: *Metaphysics* 1032ᵇ2, 1037ᵃ5, ᵃ28, ᵇ3, 1054ᵇ1, 1071ᵇ12–22. 'Others with capability': compounds of form and matter (actuality and potentiality) such as animals and other ordinary things. 'Others are never actualities': e.g. the infinite (in number or in divisibility); *Metaphysics* 1048ᵇ9–17, *Physics* III 6.

CHAPTER 14

There is no reason to doubt the Aristotelian authorship of this chapter, but it seems unlikely that it was originally written as part of the *De Interpretatione*. It is true that the conclusion in the last paragraph accords with 17ᵇ16–26 and 20ᵃ16–20, and that 23ᵃ32–35 and 24ᵇ1–2 look like references to Chapter 1. But the body of the chapter appears to argue that negations are in general the contraries of the corresponding affirmations; and this upsets the distinction between contraries and contradictories which was drawn in Chapter 7. It also conflicts with *Categories* 13ᵇ12 ff., where 'Socrates is sick' has 'Socrates is not sick' as its contradictory and 'Socrates is well' as its contrary.

23ᵃ27. Aristotle does not revert to the 'Callias' example or discuss any other singular statement. But the argument of 23ᵇ15–25 implies that it is the contradictories that are the contraries.

23^a32. 'There is a true belief about the good, that it is good': it is not clear precisely what beliefs Aristotle means to discuss. Does he want to discuss the beliefs that would be expressed by the statements 'the good is good', 'the good is not good' (!), &c.; or does he refer to beliefs expressed by statements like 'knowledge is good', 'knowledge is not good', &c. (assuming that knowledge is in fact good)? Further, are the statements in question supposed to be universal in form or indefinite?

'And if they are one belief, by reason of which is it contrary?': Aristotle is perhaps contemplating the case where one or the other of two contrary predicates must belong to a given subject (*Categories* 11^b38 ff.): to say that a number is not even is equivalent to saying that it is odd. One may still ask whether '. . . is not even' or '. . . is odd' is the correct formulation of the statement contrary to '. . . is even', reaching an answer by considering cases where there *is* a possible intermediate between contrary predicates (as there is between 'good' and 'bad', *Categories* 12^a24).

'It is false to suppose that contrary beliefs are distinguished by being of contraries': Aristotle shows that two statements with contrary predicates are not necessarily contrary. It remains to be decided whether two statements with the same subject and contrary predicates are contrary.

23^b7. Aristotle speaks of 'the belief that it is something else'. The following parenthesis seems intended to explain why in the present discussion we consider the triad '. . . is good', '. . . is not good', and '. . . is bad', and not, for example, the triad '. . . is good', '. . . is not good', and '. . . is ugly'. 'Good' and 'ugly' may be incompatible but they are not opposites.

Aristotle argues that the true belief about what a thing is in itself is more true than the true belief about what it is accidentally (or incidentally or derivatively), and that the false belief about what a thing is in itself is more false than the false belief about what it is accidentally. 'But it is he who holds the contrary belief who is most deceived', that is, holds the most false belief. Therefore it is the belief that the good is not good that is contrary to the belief that the good is good, since it is 'the false belief about what a thing is in itself'.

This is obscure and perhaps confused. It is possible to understand the suggestion that one truth may be more true than another as meaning that one true statement may entail another but not be entailed by it: '. . . is good' entails '. . . is not bad', but not conversely.

One would then expect that of two false statements that one would be the more false—the 'stronger' falsity—which entailed the other without being entailed by it: '. . . is bad' entails '. . . is not good', but not conversely. Aristotle, however, takes it that '. . . is not good' is more false than '. . . is bad' (the subject in all these cases being something good). Perhaps he has in mind the fact that 'it is false that . . . is not good' entails 'it is false that . . . is bad', but not conversely. To make the argument consistent we must then construe the statement that one true statement is more true than another, not as meaning that the one entails the other but not conversely, but as meaning that the truth of the one entails the truth of the other, but not conversely. Thus we have: if '. . . is good' is true, then '. . . is not bad' is true, but not conversely; and if '. . . is not good' is false, then 'is bad' is false, but not conversely. But it is peculiar to infer from this second implication that one who falsely believes that . . . is not good is in deeper error than one who believes that . . . is bad. The more natural way of viewing the matter is perhaps hinted at in the last sentence of the paragraph: one who believes falsely that . . . is bad necessarily believes that it is not good though that is not all that he believes (since he believes also that it is not neither good nor bad); so he is sunk in all the error of one who falsely believes that it is not good and in some extra error too.

23^b27. This paragraph assumes not only that every statement has a contrary and that the correct rule for identifying contraries is the same for all types of statement, but also that the rule is formal and guarantees that the form of the contrary of one (affirmative) statement is the same as that of any other.

24^a3. Does Aristotle tell us here that the preceding arguments hold as well for universal statements as for the non-universal statements he has been discussing, or that he has all along been meaning the statements discussed to be taken universally?

24^b1. 'For contraries are those which enclose their opposites': that is, their contradictory opposites (17^b24, 20^a19). It is natural to think of A and E as extremes and of I and O as lying between them.

NOTE ON FURTHER READING

1. *Translations*

All of Aristotle's works were included in *The Works of Aristotle translated into English*, edited by W. D. Ross (12 vols., Oxford, 1938–52). A revised version is now available in two volumes:

J. BARNES (ed.), *The Complete Works of Aristotle*, Princeton, 1984.

Reliable translations of the texts likely to be of most interest to philosophy students are contained in:

J. L. ACKRILL (ed.), *New Aristotle Reader*, Oxford and Princeton, 1987.

Volumes in the *Loeb Classical Library* (London and Cambridge, Mass.) contain Greek texts with facing translations.

2. *Books*

J. L. ACKRILL, *Aristotle the Philosopher*, Oxford, 1981.
D. J. ALLAN, *The Philosophy of Aristotle*, 2nd edn., Oxford, 1970.
J. BARNES, *Aristotle*, Oxford, 1982.
G. BRAKAS, *Aristotle's Concept of the Universal*, Hildesheim, 1988.
M. FURTH, *Substance, Form, and Psyche: an Aristotelean Metaphysics*, Cambridge, 1988.
D. W. GRAHAM, *Aristotle's Two Systems*, Oxford, 1987.
E. HARTMAN, *Substance, Body, and Soul*, Princeton, 1977.
J. HINTIKKA, *Time and Necessity*, Oxford, 1973.
T. IRWIN, *Aristotle's First Principles*, Oxford, 1988.
H. W. B. JOSEPH, *An Introduction to Logic*, 2nd edn., Oxford, 1916.
E. KAPP, *Greek Foundations of Traditional Logic*, New York, 1942.
W. KNEALE and M. KNEALE, *The Development of Logic*, Oxford, 1962.
J. LEAR, *Aristotle: the Desire to Understand*, Cambridge, 1988.
G. E. R. LLOYD, *Aristotle: the Growth and Structure of his Thought*, Cambridge, 1968.
R. H. ROBINS, *Short History of Linguistics*, London, 1967.
W. D. ROSS, *Aristotle's Metaphysics*, 2 vols., Oxford, 1924.
—— *Aristotle's Prior and Posterior Analytics*, Oxford, 1949.
—— *Aristotle*, 5th (revised) edn., London, 1953.

3. *Articles*

Reference may be made to the helpful bibliographies contained in:

J. BARNES, M. SCHOFIELD and R. SORABJI, *Articles on Aristotle* (4 vols.), London, 1975-9.

Some later work is mentioned in the 'Topics' section of:

J. L. ACKRILL, *New Aristotle Reader*, Oxford and Princeton, 1987.

GLOSSARY

ἀκολουθεῖν: 'to follow', 'to follow from' (cp. ἕπεσθαι).

ἀκολούθησις: 'implication' (literally 'following').

ἀληθής, &c.: 'true', &c.

ἀνάγκη, ἀναγκαῖον, &c.: 'necessity', 'necessary', &c.

ἀντίθεσις, ἀντικεῖσθαι, &c.: 'opposition', 'to be opposed', &c.

ἀντιστρέφειν: 'to reciprocate', 'reciprocation', 'reciprocally'.

ἀντεστραμμένως: 'conversely'.

ἀντίφασις: 'contradiction', 'contradictory pair', 'contradictories'.

ἀντιφατικῶς: 'contradictorily'.

ἀποφαίνεσθαι: 'to state', 'to make a statement'.

ἀπόφανσις: 'statement'.

ἀποφαντικός: 'statement-making' (see pp. 124-5).

ἀπόφασις, ἀποφατικός: 'negation', 'negative'.

ἀποφάναι: 'to deny'.

γένος: 'genus' (but 'kind' at 9ᵃ14, ᵃ28, 10ᵃ11).

δηλοῦν: 'to reveal'.

διάθεσις, διακεῖσθαι: 'condition', 'to be in a condition'.

διαφέρειν: 'to differ', 'to be different', &c.

διαφορά: 'differentia' (but 'difference' at 16ᵇ13, 20ᵇ33).

δόξα, &c.: 'belief', &c. (but 'thought' at 21ᵃ32-33).

δύναμις, δυνατόν: see p. 149.

εἶδος: 'species' (but 'kind' at 1ᵇ17, 8ᵇ27, 15ᵃ13, 23ᵃ6).

ἐναντίος, ἐναντιότης: 'contrary', 'contrariety'.

ἐνδέχεσθαι: see p. 149.

ἕξις: 'state' (but 'possession' in Cat. c. 10).

ἕπεσθαι: 'to follow' (cp. ἀκολουθεῖν).

ἐπιστήμη: 'knowledge', 'branch of knowledge', 'sort of knowledge' (but 'science' at 14ᵃ36-37).

κατάφασις, καταφατικός, καταφάναι: 'affirmation', 'affirmative', 'to affirm'.

κατηγορεῖν, κατηγορία: 'predicate' (but at 17ᵇ13-14 τὸ κατηγορούμενον means 'a subject'— what has something predicated of it).

κινεῖν, κίνησις, &c.: 'to change', 'change', &c. (cp. μεταβάλλειν).

λόγος: see p. 124.

μεταβάλλειν, μεταβολή, &c.: 'to change', 'change', &c. (cp. κινεῖν).

ὁμώνυμος, ὁμωνύμως: 'homonymous', 'homonymously'.

ὄνομα: 'name' (see p. 115).

οὐσία: 'substance' (but 'being' in Cat. c. 1).

πάσχειν, πάθος, &c.: 'to be affected', 'affection', &c.

παρώνυμος, παρωνύμως: 'paronymous', 'paronymously'.

πρᾶγμα: 'actual thing' (see p. 122).

πτῶσις: 'ending' (1ᵃ13, 6ᵇ33), 'inflexion' (16ᵇ1, ᵇ17, 17ᵃ10).

ῥῆμα: 'verb' (see p. 118).

σημεῖον, σημαίνειν, σημαντικός, &c.: 'sign', 'signify', 'significant'.

στέρησις, ἐστερῆσθαι: 'privation', 'to be deprived'.

συμβεβηκός: 'accidental'.

κατὰ συμβεβηκός: 'accidentally' (but 'derivatively' at 5ᵃ39, ᵇ10).

σύμβολον : 'symbol'.

συμπλοκή : 'combination' (but 'compound' at 21ᵃ5) (cp. σύνθεσις).

συμπλεκόμενα : (21ᵃ38) 'combined'.

συμπεπλεγμένη : (23ᵇ25) 'complex'.

πεπλεγμένα : (16ᵃ24) 'complex', (21ᵃ1) 'compounded'.

σύνθεσις : 'combination' (cp. συμπλοκή).

σύνθετος : (17ᵃ22) 'composite'.

συντιθέμενα : (20ᵇ31) 'in combination'.

συγκείμενον : 'compounded', 'component', &c.

συνωνυμος, συνωνύμως : 'synonymous', 'synonymously'.

τρόπος : 'way' or 'manner'.

ὑποκείμενον, ὑποκεῖσθαι : 'subject', 'to be a subject' (literally 'to underlie').

φάσις : 'expression' (but 'affirmation' at 21ᵇ21).

φωνή : 'spoken sound', 'spoken' (but 'utterance' at 17ᵃ18).

ψευδής, &c. : 'false', &c.

INDEX OF SUBJECTS

Lightning Source UK Ltd.
Milton Keynes UK
UKOW02f0247020914

237918UK00001B/45/A